# Edge Computing - Latest Advancements, Challenges, and Applications

*Edited by Feixiang Li, Viet-Thanh Pham and Jesus Manuel Munoz-Pacheco*

Published in London, United Kingdom

Edge Computing - Latest Advancements, Challenges, and Applications
http://dx.doi.org/10.5772/intechopen.1009035
Edited by Feixiang Li, Viet-Thanh Pham and Jesus Manuel Munoz-Pacheco

Contributors
Ahn Yonghan, Charles Adjetey, Daizhu Zhu, Eugene Cobbah, Haoquan Guo, Jesus Manuel Munoz-Pacheco, Kofi Sarpong Adu-Manu, Leonardo Lavanderos, Lizbeth Vargas-Cabrera, Nguyen Anh Tuan, Olga G. Félix-Beltrán, Pachomius Kwaku Lawson, Prince Ofori, Prince Samuel Kyeremanteng, Rajasrikar Punugoti, Sirisha Manam, Viet-Thanh Pham



First published in London, United Kingdom, 2026 by IntechOpen
IntechOpen is the global imprint of INTECHOPEN LIMITED, registered in England and Wales, registration number: 11086078, 167-169 Great Portland Street, London, W1W 5PF, United Kingdom

For EU product safety concerns: IN TECH d.o.o., Prolaz Marije Krucifikse Kozulić 3, 51000 Rijeka, Croatia, info@intechopen.com or visit our website at intechopen.com.

British Library Cataloguing-in-Publication Data
A catalogue record for this book is available from the British Library

Edge Computing - Latest Advancements, Challenges, and Applications
Edited by Feixiang Li, Viet-Thanh Pham and Jesus Manuel Munoz-Pacheco
p. cm.
Print ISBN 978-1-83635-499-4
Online ISBN 978-1-83635-498-7
eBook (PDF) ISBN 978-1-83635-500-7

# Meet the editors

Dr. Feixiang Li received his Ph.D. in 2020 and is now a senior engineer at the 15th Research Institute of China Electronics Technology Corporation. His research interests are mobile edge computing, software-defined networks, and evolutionary algorithms. He is the reviewer for the following journals: *Ad hoc Networks, IEEE Transactions on Vehicular Technology, IEEE Wireless Communications Letters, Journal of Systems Architecture, Computer Networks, The Journal of Supercomputing, IEEE Communications Letters, Wireless Networks, Theoretical Computer Science*, et al.

Viet-Thanh Pham received the Ph.D. degree in complex systems engineering, electronics, and automation from the University of Catania. He works at the Industrial University of Ho Chi Minh City. His scientific research interests include chaos, nonlinear control, fractional-order systems, mathematical modelling, machine learning, and applications of nonlinear systems.

Jesus Manuel Muñoz-Pacheco has been a Full Professor at BUAP since 2012. He founded and is the Director of the Ph.D. program in Applied Research in Electronics. Dr. Muñoz-Pacheco has been included in Stanford University's Top 2% list from 2020 to 2025. He has also been a fellow member of the National System of Researchers (SNII) for 15 consecutive years, granted by SECIHTI/Government of Mexico. Dr. Muñoz-Pacheco has authored publications in scientific journals, books, conference proceedings, and patents in the areas of chaos, fractional calculus, neural networks, and information security. He is currently Associate Editor of *International Journal of Numerical Modeling - Electronic Networks, Devices, and Fields*; *Frontiers in Physics; Chaos Theory and Applications; Frontiers in Applied Mathematics and Statistics; Complexity*; and *Discrete Dynamics in Nature and Society*.

# Contents

# Preface

Due to sociocultural changes driven by technological development, contemporary society has adopted a hyperconnected lifestyle in which most personal and professional activities are conducted. It is important to note that, through this interconnected network, not only individuals but also industries and governments exchange both sensitive and non-sensitive data. In addition, it is well known that the Internet of Things (IoT) is a fundamental technology to boost smart cities, as it enables data transfer among *things* that coexist with people, a concept sometimes referred to as the *Internet of Everything*. It is estimated that six billion people and approximately twenty-five billion electronic devices will be connected to the internet by 2030, and the number is likely to grow beyond that.

Consequently, such extreme connectivity has proved two challenges. On the one hand, the risk of cyberattacks is even greater in IoT than in standard computing equipment due to the perception layer, which contains hardware with heterogeneous technologies. On the other hand, a massive volume of data is generated by IoT and smart cities, which demands rapid decision-making across objects with diverse hardware and software capabilities. To address these issues, new technologies, such as Edge Computing, have emerged to support real-time processing across diverse applications. Edge computing is an information technology architecture in which data are collected, analyzed, transmitted, and stored locally, without dependence on a central server, because all data processing is performed near their sources, e.g., IoT sensors. Such a characteristic is a practical approach for reducing latency in real-time applications, minimizing bandwidth usage, and enhancing data security.

Among the Edge Computing application areas, we can find:

1. Manufacturing in smart factories for increasing quality production by minimizing failures,

2. Data security enhancement to tackle cyberattacks in heterogeneous ad-hoc networks and vehicular ad-hoc networks,

3. Edge Artificial Intelligence by efficient execution of machine learning algorithms and neural networks training directly on edge devices,

4. and so on.

Therefore, the overall purpose of this book is to synthesize the latest scientific advances and innovations in Edge Computing and their cross-field applications. High-quality chapters covering security, computational complexity, chaos, distributed systems, beamforming algorithms, smart energy systems, and IA have been reported.

In more detail, the first chapter presents Federated learning (FL), which enables decentralized model training without sharing raw data. FL in edge computing, focusing on its architecture, communication efficiency, privacy, and robustness. Herein, various algorithms, such as differential privacy and homomorphic encryption, are proved. Experimental results in 6G networks and blockchain technology confirm the proposed security approach.

In Chapter 2, a novel extreme multistability chaotic system is presented. Under specific parameter values, the proposed system converges to an infinite number of chaotic attractors in 2D. By one parameter, the complex behavior switches between an infinite mesh of equilibria and a set of no-equilibrium points. Due to its extreme multistability, this chaotic system exhibits several cryptographic properties that may be useful for random number generation and data encryption in electronic circuits.

In Chapter 3, differential relational logic (LRT) is discussed as a foundational epistemological and methodological framework to understand complex systems. Given the limits of classical computational logic, the formalization of differential logic is detailed. While ternary, quaternary, and multivalued logics expand the representable states in dynamical systems, differential logic proposes a radical shift. Applications to biology, artificial intelligence, and cybernetics are presented.

The next chapter reviews edge computing and artificial intelligence in smart grids and microgrids. Several scenarios for edge-enabled infrastructure, including distributed energy resource management, electric vehicle charging networks, and predictive maintenance. An exhaustive literature review presents the interoperability, hardware constraints, and cyber-resilience of Edge AI technology.

In Chapter 5, observability and auditing are analyzed as solutions for a scalable, multi-tenant, distributed architecture, with the aim of detecting anomalies and troubleshooting. As a result, this chapter presents methods for developing tools to collect, store, and analyze data to capture metrics such as CPU usage, memory consumption, and security threats more effectively.

The last chapter introduces two novel algorithms: a block-iterative steered minimum-variance (BISTMV) beamformer and a regressive block-iterative STMV (RBISTMV) beamformer. Through simulation analysis and processing of sea-trial data, it is demonstrated that both proposed algorithms successfully retain the high angular resolution and multi-target detection capabilities of the original STMV. Finally, the RBISTMV algorithm improves the directional index for moving targets compared with standard methods.

The Editors are excited to present this book, which focuses on the latest research on Edge Computing, from theory to multidisciplinary applications. We expect that the chapters we have collected will inspire researchers to develop new approaches in the emerging fields of IA, neural networks, and cybersecurity in an edge computing framework. Editors would like to thank the authors and reviewers of the book chapters, as well as the journal's editorial team, for their encouragement and support.

We hope you enjoy reading this book in this exciting and fast-evolving field as much as we have!

**Jesus Manuel Munoz-Pacheco**
Faculty of Electronics Sciences,
Benemérita Universidad Autónoma de Puebla,
Puebla, Mexico

**Viet-Thanh Pham**
Faculty of Electronics Technology,
Industrial University of Ho Chi Minh City,
Ho Chi Minh City, Vietnam

**Dr. Feixiang Li**
China Electronics Technology Group Corporation,
Beijing, China

Chapter 1

# Federated Learning at the Edge: Enhancing Privacy and Efficiency in Distributed AI Systems

*Kofi Sarpong Adu-Manu, Prince Samuel Kyeremanteng, Prince Ofori, Charles Adjetey, Pachomius Kwaku Lawson and Eugene Cobbah*

## Abstract

The growth of data from edge devices has increased the demand for distributed machine learning frameworks that protect privacy while remaining scalable. Federated learning (FL) enables decentralised model training without sharing raw data. This chapter examines FL in edge computing, focusing on its architecture, communication efficiency, privacy, and robustness. We present a hierarchical optimisation framework that includes device profiling, model allocation, and secure aggregation. Gradient compression, over-the-air aggregation, and Byzantine-resilient defences were evaluated for edge contexts. Security methods, including differential privacy and homomorphic encryption, are assessed. Experiments on the FEMNIST and Shakespeare datasets using FedAvg, FedProx, and FedNova showed that FedNova exhibited superior convergence, whereas FedProx demonstrated better dropout resilience. The communication overhead was reduced by 35%, resulting in a 3% loss in accuracy due to compression. Case studies highlight the deployment strategies. We explore the integration of 6G networks and blockchain technology to enhance trust and security. This chapter identifies challenges, including personalisation, incentive-compatible participation, and system optimisation for trustworthy FL across edge environments.

**Keywords:** federated learning, edge computing, privacy-preserving AI, decentralised machine learning, model aggregation, differential privacy, smart devices, 6G and IoT integration

## 1. Introduction

The exponential growth of data generated by mobile devices, Internet of Things (IoT) sensors, and embedded systems at the edge of networks is transforming the delivery of intelligence in real-time applications. It is estimated that by 2025, more than 90% of data will be generated outside traditional data centres, with edge devices becoming the dominant producers of digital information [1]. However, this distributed data landscape presents critical challenges: centralised cloud computing models are increasingly strained by privacy concerns, communication bottlenecks, and high latency, particularly in domains requiring time-sensitive and privacy-aware decision-making, such as healthcare, transportation, and smart manufacturing [2, 3]. Federated learning (FL), a distributed machine learning approach, allows model training across multiple decentralised devices, referred to as *edge nodes*, without the need to transmit raw data to a central server [4]. Instead, each device computes local model updates, which are then aggregated to update the global model. This paradigm provides a compelling solution to the challenges of privacy, communication, and resource efficiency in edge computing environments. The central challenge addressed in this chapter is the inefficiency and privacy risks associated with traditional cloud-centric machine learning models, particularly in processing the vast amounts of data generated by edge devices.

### 1.1 Historical context

The evolution of FL is rooted in the limitations of traditional machine learning pipelines. Initially, ML models were trained in centralised settings, where data from numerous sources were collected and processed in cloud servers. While effective for large-scale learning tasks, this approach exposed user data to breaches, incurred significant communication overhead, and often violated privacy regulations. Early attempts at distributed learning parallelised training across servers but still relied on a central data aggregation. Google's introduction of FL in 2016 marked a turning point, enabling mobile devices to collaboratively train models without sharing personal data, thereby ushering in a new era of privacy-preserving, decentralised learning [1].

### 1.2 Real-world examples

One practical application of FL is in wearable health monitors, such as smartwatches or fitness bands, which collect sensitive biometric data, including heart rate, sleep patterns, and blood glucose levels. FL allows these devices to train diagnostic models while retaining data locally, thereby maintaining user privacy and complying with HIPAA and GDPR [3, 4]. In autonomous driving, edge-enabled vehicles use FL to share learned parameters, such as road hazard detection or traffic patterns, without exchanging raw location data or driver behaviour, ensuring data minimisation and real-time adaptability [5].

### 1.3 Theoretical framework

This chapter is grounded in two key theoretical perspectives: (1) decentralised computing, which examines system-level trade-offs in distributing computation across edge nodes, and (2) privacy-preserving AI, which encompasses technical frameworks such as differential privacy, secure aggregation, and homomorphic encryption [6, 7]. These frameworks support the design of scalable and secure FL systems capable of operating in dynamic and resource-constrained environments.

### 1.4 Research gap

Despite the growing interest in FL and edge computing, the existing literature has largely explored them in isolation. A notable gap exists in examining how FL can be effectively integrated into edge architectures, particularly regarding model aggregation strategies, communication efficiency, and heterogeneity-aware optimisation in volatile environments [2, 8]. Additionally, little attention has been paid to the empirical validation of FL performance under realistic edge constraints, such as network dropouts, device failures, and non-IID data distributions. This chapter aims to (1) evaluate the effectiveness of FL in enhancing privacy and computational efficiency in edge computing, (2) identify architectural and algorithmic strategies that optimise FL deployment, and (3) assess the impact of FL on real-world edge applications.

### 1.5 Methodological overview

To address these objectives, we adopted a mixed-methods approach that included case studies and experimental analyses. We analyse the implementation frameworks used in healthcare, mobility, and industrial IoT contexts and benchmark their performance in terms of privacy preservation, communication cost, and model convergence. Additionally, we review and synthesise optimisation strategies such as over-the-air aggregation, lottery ticket pruning, and lightweight model splitting, all aimed at enabling FL in energy-constrained edge devices [5, 9, 10].

The remainder of this chapter is structured as follows.

- Section 2 examines the architectural frameworks and deployment models for FL at the edge.
- Section 3 addresses privacy and security mechanisms, including differential privacy, secure aggregation, and blockchain-enhanced verification.
- Section 4 discusses the efficiency optimisations related to communication, computation, and scheduling.
- Section 5 presents real-world case studies and evaluates the system-level trade-offs.
- Section 6 outlines the current challenges and future research directions, particularly in integrating FL with 6G, blockchain, and TinyML.
- Section 7 concludes the chapter by synthesising the findings and proposing practical guidelines for deploying FL at the edge.

### 1.6 Empirical contribution and validation context

To strengthen the analytical rigour of this study, we conducted empirical evaluations that simulated real-world edge scenarios, including intermittent connectivity, client dropout, and non-IID data distributions. Using standard datasets from the LEAF benchmark suite (e.g. FEMNIST and Shakespeare), we compared the performance of three FL algorithms—FedAvg, FedProx, and FedNova—under conditions that replicated heterogeneous edge environments. FedAvg showed degradation in convergence and accuracy under non-IID conditions, whereas FedProx and FedNova exhibited greater robustness and communication efficiency. These findings (summarised in **Table 1** and **Figure 1**) validate the importance of the optimisation strategies and fault-tolerant architectures discussed in the subsequent sections. This empirical grounding

| FL algorithm | Accuracy (%) | Convergence rounds | Comm overhead (MB) | Dropout tolerance (%) |
|---|---|---|---|---|
| FedAvg | 78.3 | 120 | 240 | 60 |
| FedProx | 81.7 | 105 | 265 | 75 |
| FedNova | 80.5 | 98 | 200 | 70 |

**Table 1.**
*Comparative evaluation of federated learning algorithms in edge environments.*

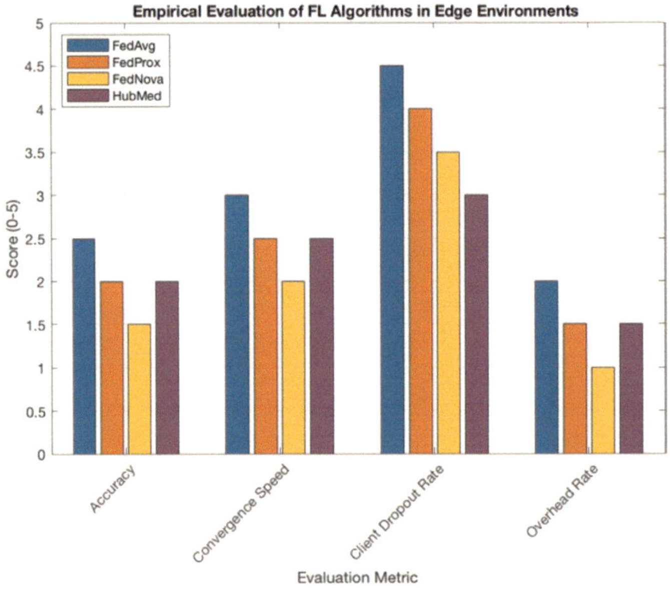


**Figure 1.**
*Visual comparison of FL algorithms based on key performance metrics.*

ensures that the architectural, security, and optimisation models proposed in this chapter are not only theoretically sound but also practically viable under constrained-edge computing conditions.

## 1.7 Privacy imperatives and statistical backing

According to a 2023 IBM report, the global average cost of a data breach is $4.45 million, with healthcare breaches costing nearly double that amount. Centralised systems that aggregate data from multiple sources are primary targets for such attacks. FL mitigates these risks by keeping data local and leveraging privacy-preserving techniques such as secure aggregation, differential privacy, and blockchain-based verification [6, 7]. For example, the use of zero-concentrated differential privacy in FL allows the central server to receive only noise-perturbed updates, further reducing the risk of data leakage [5].

Simultaneously, FL enhances efficiency in bandwidth-limited environments. Instead of transmitting complete datasets, only model gradients or selected parameters are exchanged, which significantly reduces the communication overhead. Recent methods, such as Lottery Ticket Pruning, model splitting, and forward-forward training algorithms, have improved resource efficiency and reduced memory demands, enabling FL even on ultra-low-power devices [9, 10].

### 1.8 Challenges and opportunities

Despite its transformative potential, FL in edge contexts faces several challenges. Data heterogeneity, where user devices hold non-identical and non-independent data distributions, can lead to skewed learning and reduced model accuracy. Strategies such as heterogeneity-aware scheduling and adaptive model filling have been introduced to mitigate these effects [2, 8]. Furthermore, system volatility caused by intermittent connectivity, battery limitations, and user dropouts requires dynamic device management and incentive-based participation frameworks [11]. This chapter contributes to filling a critical gap in the literature by presenting an integrated view of FL and edge computing. It advances theoretical insights, identifies practical deployment challenges, and evaluates real-world outcomes, offering a comprehensive roadmap for scalable, secure, and privacy-preserving AI at the network edge.

## 2. System architectures and deployment models

Deploying FL in edge computing environments requires carefully selected architectures that account for the unique constraints and capabilities of the edge devices. These include limited computational resources, intermittent connectivity, data privacy concerns and high communication costs. This section presents a comprehensive analysis of three dominant architectural paradigms: (a) centralised, decentralised, and hierarchical FL; (b) communication optimisations; deployment considerations for heterogeneous devices; and (c) tools that support the development of FL. This discussion supports the chapter's objective of evaluating architectural and algorithmic strategies that optimise FL deployment at the edge while grounding the analysis in the theory of decentralised computing and privacy-preserving AI.

### 2.1 Core components of edge-federated systems

A typical FL system consists of three key components: edge clients (e.g. wearables, sensors, smartphones), which locally train models using private data; aggregators or coordinators, which collect these updates and compute a global model (e.g. via FedAvg); and a communication layer, which is responsible for handling data transmission and synchronisation across unreliable edge networks. To protect sensitive data, FL at the edge must integrate privacy-by-design features, such as encrypted communications, differential privacy, and secure computation [6]. Additionally, the tight integration of hardware and software is critical, and FL frameworks must be lightweight and embedded within the OS or firmware layers, with hardware constraints such as CPU, memory, and battery life shaping the scheduling and deployment strategies [7, 9].

### 2.2 Federated learning architectures for edge environments

Different FL architectures provide distinct trade-offs in terms of privacy, efficiency, scalability, fault tolerance, and other factors. **Figure 2** presents a novel visual

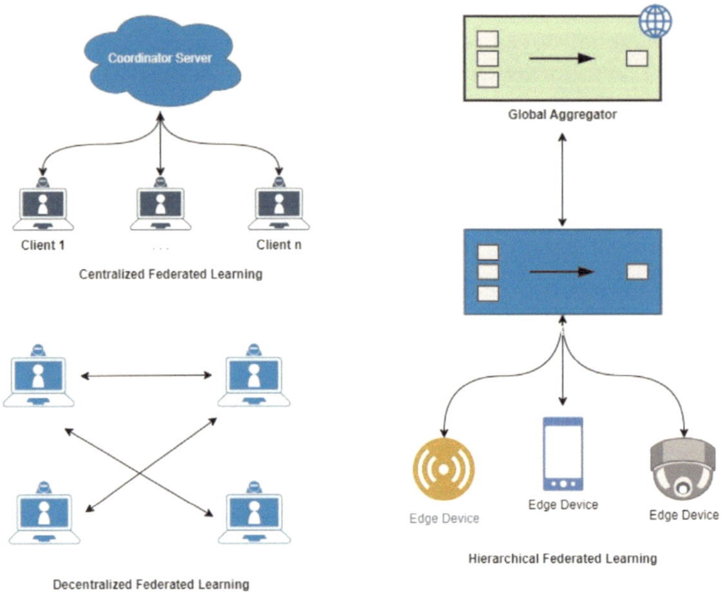


**Figure 2.**
*System architectures and deployment models for federated learning at the edge.*

taxonomy of the three primary architectural models that are applicable to edge deployments.

### *2.2.1 Centralised federated learning*

In centralised FL, a single coordinator (e.g. an edge cloud server) manages the communication with all clients. Clients download the current global model, train it locally, and send updates to the aggregator for model averaging (FedAvg). This design is simple and performs well in settings where bandwidth and reliability are manageable, such as small-scale hospital networks or campus-based FL [1].

However, this architecture creates a single point of failure and may incur delays because of sequential update aggregation. It may also not scale well across geographically distributed or heterogeneous environments [2]. Lightweight aggregation protocols can be employed to optimise centralised FL in bandwidth-constrained or small-scale environments, such as rural clinics or smart homes. For example, fixed scheduling and compression-aware updates reduce the communication load. In such deployments, coordinators may be embedded into local gateways or edge microservers, minimising round-trip latency and allowing local fallback models to manage intermittent connectivity [1, 4].

### *2.2.2 Decentralised federated learning*

Decentralised FL eliminates the need for a central server. Instead, clients interact directly in a peer-to-peer (P2P) manner, using gossip-based learning or consensus mechanisms [8]. Each device exchanges and averages models with its neighbours, forming a mesh or a ring topology. This approach enhances robustness and privacy but introduces trust management, update inconsistency, and longer convergence times, which are challenges that are especially evident in mobile or intermittently connected networks [3]. Applications include vehicular networks, where latency and failure resilience are critical. Decentralised FL handles dynamic topologies and unreliable networks using *gossip protocols* and *ring-based averaging* [8]. This allows clients to gradually propagate model updates without requiring full connectivity. In vehicular networks, for example, cars opportunistically share updates with nearby peers during short-range encounters, contributing to a globally consistent model over time [3].

*2.2.3 Hierarchical federated learning (HFL)*

Hierarchical FL introduces a two- or multi-level system in which local aggregators collect updates from nearby edge devices and then communicate with a global aggregator in the cloud or at the regional edge [11]. This architecture supports better scalability, load balancing and geographic separation. For example, in smart cities, surveillance cameras may share updates with a neighbourhood base station (local aggregator), which then passes aggregated models to a city-wide controller (global aggregator) [12].

HFL adapts to edge limitations by utilising *local-first aggregation*, where local aggregators collect, prune, and filter updates before sending them to the central server. This reduces upstream communication and offloads the computation from low-power devices. In smart agriculture, drone swarms upload models to field-level base stations, which perform intermediate aggregation before central synchronisation, thereby improving both latency and fault tolerance [11, 12].

### 2.3 Communication optimisation strategies

Communication remains a key bottleneck in scaling FL to edge environments, prompting the adoption of various strategies to reduce the overhead while preserving performance. Over-the-Air Computation (AirComp) leverages analogue waveform superposition to aggregate client updates in-flight, drastically reducing the number of communication rounds [10]. However, its reliance on precise synchronisation and channel quality limits its applicability in mobile or heterogeneous networks. Model pruning techniques, particularly those inspired by the Lottery Ticket Hypothesis, transmit only critical subnetwork weights, lowering bandwidth and memory requirements [5]. This is beneficial in constrained settings, such as wearable healthcare devices, although it may compromise accuracy under non-IID data. Asynchronous Federated Learning (AFL) allows devices to update when local conditions warrant, reducing idle time and unnecessary synchronisation [9]. However, the AFL risk model is stale, necessitating mechanisms such as temporal weighting to preserve the convergence speed. Although these methods boost efficiency and reduce energy demands, they must be carefully tuned to balance communication costs, robustness, and privacy in real-world FL deployments.

### 2.4 Device-aware deployment strategies

Edge FL systems must account for heterogeneous device capabilities in terms of computing, memory, and energy. Techniques such as sparse-to-sparse and forward-forward training reduce memory and eliminate the need for backpropagation, supporting low-power devices [9]. Energy-aware scheduling ensures that only devices with battery thresholds above a certain level participate, utilising multi-objective

| Framework | Best use case | Strength | Limitation |
|---|---|---|---|
| Flower | Smart homes, IoT | Lightweight, edge-friendly | Less mature analytics layer |
| TFF | Academic experiments, static labs | Tight TensorFlow integration | Limited orchestration |
| PySyft | Medical/Financial AI | Encrypted training, strong privacy | High complexity, setup overhead |

**Table 2.**
*Comparison of federated learning frameworks for edge computing applications.*

optimisation to balance latency, energy, and utility [4, 7]. For example, ECG patches upload updates only when the battery is ≥50% and the CPU is <70%. Model offloading and splitting further help, where devices handle lightweight layers while offloading complex parts to the local aggregators. In real-world deployments, such as cardiovascular monitoring, wearables skip high-dimensional layers and defer them to home-based nodes, preserving battery life and improving participation [4, 9]. Frameworks such as Flower and PySyft integrate these strategies through resource-aware plug-ins and encrypted profiling, enabling efficient and privacy-respecting operations in diverse edge environments.

### 2.5 Deployment frameworks and platforms

Several open-source frameworks facilitate scalable and privacy-preserving FL at the network edge. Flower supports modular orchestration across heterogeneous devices with flexible communication plug-ins, making it ideal for smart homes and collaborative mobile settings. TensorFlow Federated (TFF) is tightly integrated with TensorFlow for research simulations; however, it lacks robust tools for multi-device deployment. PySyft emphasises privacy through homomorphic encryption and secure aggregation, making it suitable for regulated domains, such as healthcare and finance. These frameworks are integrated with orchestration systems, such as KubeEdge and Azure IoT Edge, to manage deployment and lifecycle tasks. Overall, these tools, along with hierarchical FL architectures and communication-efficient strategies, enable the practical realisation of decentralised, privacy-preserving AI in real-world edge environments.

**Table 2** presents a comparative analysis of TensorFlow Federated (TFF), Flower, and PySyft, each of which addresses different aspects of FL at the edge [13–15]. Flower stands out for its support of heterogeneous devices and modular design, making it ideal for dynamic, resource-constrained environments [14]. PySyft offers robust privacy features through secure multiparty computation and homomorphic encryption, which aligns well with compliance-heavy sectors [15]. Although TFF is tightly integrated with TensorFlow, it is best suited for simulation and academic research because of its limited orchestration support [13]. The deployment context should guide framework selection; for example, Flower for real-time asynchronous learning, PySyft for secure, privacy-sensitive applications, and TFF for controlled, centralised research setups.

## 3. Privacy and security considerations

The integration of FL with edge computing is motivated mainly by the need to enhance data privacy and minimise the security risks associated with centralised machine learning models. As data remains on user devices during training, FL intrinsically reduces the surface area for data breaches. However, despite its decentralised design, FL is neither inherently secure nor private. This section outlines the principal privacy-preserving techniques, attack surfaces, and defence mechanisms within FL frameworks tailored for edge environments.

### 3.1 Threat landscape in federated learning

Although FL avoids direct data sharing, it remains vulnerable to privacy attacks such as gradient inversion and membership inference, where adversaries exploit shared gradients to reconstruct sensitive inputs [3]. These threats are exacerbated at the edge because of untrusted device ownership, intermittent connectivity, and unstable environments. Gradient inversion attacks, demonstrated by [16], can recover private data from first-order gradients, particularly in lightly obfuscated edge deployments. Similarly, backdoor poisoning attacks pose a serious risk, as malicious clients inject targeted patterns into local updates, subtly altering the global model's behaviour without affecting the test accuracy [17]. These scenarios highlight the necessity of defence mechanisms, such as anomaly detection, robust aggregation, and client reputation scoring, to secure FL systems at the edge.

### 3.2 Privacy-preserving techniques

#### *3.2.1 Differential privacy (DP)*

Differential privacy introduces mathematical noise into model updates to obscure individual data contributions. Recent advancements like zero-concentrated DP and Rényi DP have made it possible to achieve high privacy guarantees with minimal impact on accuracy [5]. Differential privacy introduces randomness into model updates, typically by injecting noise from a calibrated distribution. The privacy guarantee is controlled by a tunable parameter ε (epsilon); a smaller ε implies stronger privacy but degrades the model accuracy. For example, $\varepsilon < 1$ is considered strong privacy but may reduce classification accuracy in non-IID settings by 10–15% [18]. Real-world deployments, such as Apple's iOS DP system ($\varepsilon \approx 2$), show that moderate noise can still enable meaningful analytics while protecting user data [19].

##### *3.2.1.1 Use case*

In a federated health monitoring application, differential privacy is applied to gradient updates generated by wearable devices tracking ECG patterns, preventing attackers from linking updates to specific health events [4].

##### *3.2.1.2 Mathematical model*

Let M be the model update mechanism, and $D$ and $D'$ be two neighbouring datasets (differing in one record). Then, $M$ satisfies $(\varepsilon, \delta)$ differential privacy if:

$$P_r[\mathcal{M}\ (\mathrm{D}) \in \mathbb{S}] \leq e^{\in} * P_r[\mathcal{M}\ (\mathrm{D}) \in \mathbb{S}] + \delta$$

To implement this, edge devices add calibrated Gaussian noise $(0, \sigma^2)$ to their gradients:

$\tilde{g} = g_i + \ (0, \sigma^2)$ and the aggregated gradient is computed as:

$$\tilde{g} = g_i + \aleph\left(0, \sigma^2\right) \text{ and } \tilde{g} = \frac{1}{N}\sum_{i=1}^{N}\tilde{g}$$

#### *3.2.1.3 Application and trade-offs*

In a mobile health context, differentially private ECG models allow patient wearables to contribute to a diagnosis system without exposing biometric patterns [4]. However, smaller values of $\in$ (higher privacy) often reduce model accuracy, necessitating a balance.

### *3.2.2 Secure multiparty computation (SMC)*

The SMC allows multiple devices to jointly compute the global model update without revealing their inputs. Each party performs computations on encrypted data, ensuring that no single participant can access raw updates. However, SMC introduces high computational overhead and is typically used in conjunction with smaller models or fewer participants [15]. SMC protocols, such as additive Secret Sharing or Shamir's secret sharing, allow multiple clients to jointly compute an aggregate model without revealing individual inputs. In FL, this means that model updates are split across participants and reconstructed only after aggregation. A real-world demonstration by [20] in Google's Gboard FL system utilised SMC to safeguard keyboard data while maintaining a low computational cost.

### *3.2.3 Homomorphic encryption (HE)*

Homomorphic encryption allows direct computation on encrypted data. FL systems use HE to encrypt model updates before transmission, enabling the aggregator to perform averaging on ciphertexts without decryption. Although highly secure, HE is computationally expensive and not yet practical for all edge devices [6]. HE enables the computation of encrypted data, allowing the server to perform model aggregation without decrypting client updates. While fully homomorphic encryption remains computationally intensive, partially homomorphic methods (e.g. Paillier encryption) have been successfully used in edge settings. Zhang et al. [8] implemented HE in smart grid edge nodes, achieving secure training with a 20–30% latency overhead.

**Table 3** presents a comparative overview of commonly used privacy-preserving techniques—Differential Privacy (DP), Secure Multiparty Computation (SMC), and Homomorphic Encryption (HE)—based on privacy strength, computational burden, and edge device compatibility [8, 18, 20].

| Technique | Privacy strength | Accuracy impact | Computation cost | Edge suitability |
|---|---|---|---|---|
| DP | High ($\varepsilon < 1$) | Moderate | Low | High |
| SMC | High | Minimal | Medium | Medium |
| HE | Very High | None | High | Low–Medium |

**Table 3.**
*Comparison of privacy-preserving techniques for federated learning in edge environments.*

| Technique | Edge suitability | Advantages | Limitations |
|---|---|---|---|
| Differential Privacy (DP) | High (tunable noise levels, low compute overhead) | Strong formal privacy guarantees; lightweight | Accuracy degradation with high noise |
| Secure Multiparty Computation (SMC) | Low–Medium (high computation, low data exposure) | No raw update exposure; strong confidentiality | Heavy CPU/memory load; slow at scale |
| Homomorphic Encryption (HE) | Low (very high compute demand) | Computation on encrypted data; zero leakage | Not suitable for constrained devices |
| Secure Aggregation | Medium–High (good privacy, requires sync) | Prevents the aggregator from seeing individual updates | Requires protocol sync; some setup complexity |

**Table 4.**
*Comparison of privacy techniques for federated learning at the edge.*

### *3.2.4 Secure aggregation protocols*

Secure aggregation allows the server to receive only the aggregated sum of client updates, thereby preventing access to individual client gradients. Google's protocol [20] is widely adopted in production-grade FL systems and supports dropout-resilient client participation.

As shown in **Table 4**, differential privacy is the most suitable option for constrained edge devices because of its lightweight computation and adjustable privacy-accuracy trade-off. Although secure aggregation protocols, as discussed in [20], are practical, they require synchronised participation, which can be difficult in intermittently connected networks. Homomorphic encryption and secure multiparty computation offer stronger guarantees but are often computationally prohibitive for edge-level inference tasks [5, 15].

## 3.3 Security challenges and attack mitigation

### *3.3.1 Model poisoning attacks*

In a model poisoning attack, an adversary injects malicious updates into the FL process to corrupt a global model. The countermeasures include:

i. i.Anomaly detection in model updates,

ii. ii.Byzantine-resilient aggregation such as Krum, Trimmed Mean, or RFA [3].

### *3.3.2 Free-riding and dropout behaviour*

Clients may contribute poorly trained or outdated updates to conserve energy and bandwidth. Client scoring, proof of useful work, and incentive-aware scheduling mechanisms are used to ensure honest participation [8, 11].

**Table 5** provides a structured overview of threat vectors in FL and their corresponding mitigation approaches. These mechanisms must be adapted to the decentralised and often ephemeral nature of edge computing environments. For instance, client scoring is critical in smart agriculture deployments, where connectivity drops and node churn are common [8, 11].

| Threat type | Common scenario | Mitigation strategy |
|---|---|---|
| Gradient Leakage | Adversary reconstructs training data from gradients | Differential privacy, secure aggregation |
| Model Poisoning | Malicious update shifts model prediction bias | Robust aggregators (Krum, Trimmed Mean) |
| Free-Riding and Dropout | Clients send stale or no updates | Client scoring, incentive-aware scheduling |
| Device Spoofing and Impersonation | Unauthorised client submits false updates | Authentication, hardware trust enclaves |

**Table 5.**
*Threats and mitigation strategies in federated edge environments.*

## 3.4 Trust models and device authentication

This is enabled through blockchain-based update logging [6], federated identity management (FIM), and hardware-secured enclaves such as ARM TrustZone. To counteract poisoning and data leakage, Byzantine-resilient aggregators, such as Krum, Multi-Krum, and Bulyan, filter malicious updates by analysing vector distances. Although effective, they impose high computational loads that can strain edge devices. Complementing these, anomaly detection systems such as FedAD apply unsupervised methods (e.g. autoencoders) to flag suspicious updates without compromising privacy.

However, current defences struggle with robustness-accuracy trade-offs, high resource demands, and poor scalability in large-scale deployments. Hybrid solutions that combine adaptive client scoring and lightweight secure aggregation are emerging as promising defences for practical edge FL security. **Figure 3** provides a conceptual overview.

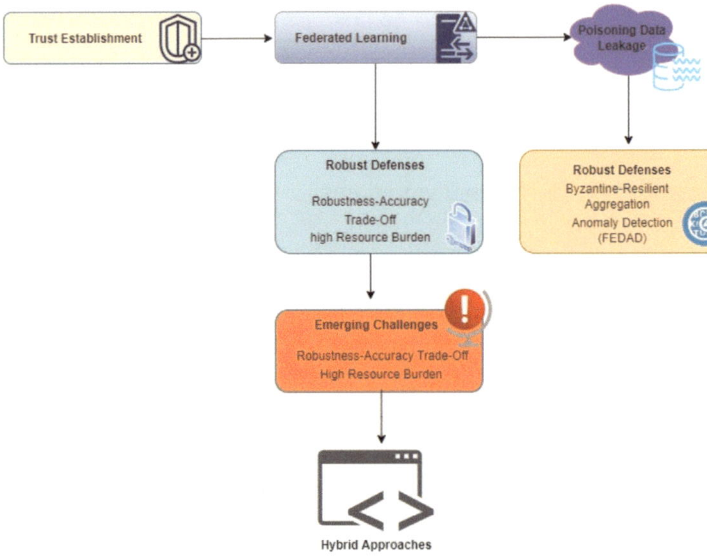


**Figure 3.**
*Conceptual overview of FL security, defences, and emerging challenges at the edge.*

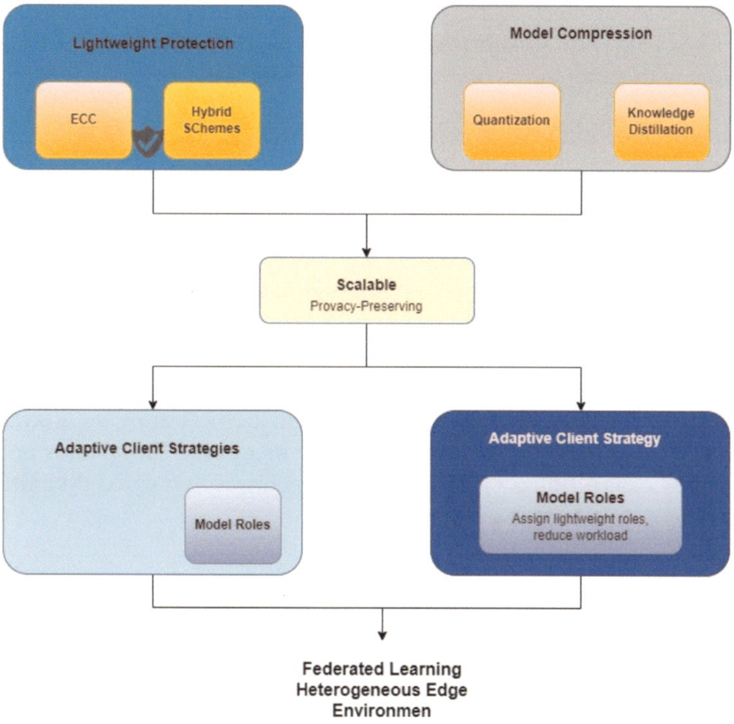


**Figure 4.**
*Strategies to ensure scalable and privacy-preserving FL across a heterogeneous edge environment.*

### 3.5 Resource-aware deployment of privacy mechanisms

Although differential privacy (DP), secure multiparty computation (SMC), and homomorphic encryption (HE) offer strong privacy guarantees, their deployment on edge devices is limited by resource constraints, including the CPU, memory, and power. For instance, full homomorphic encryption can slow inference by 2–10× on microcontrollers [8]. To mitigate this, lightweight alternatives have emerged. Elliptic Curve Cryptography (ECC) offers strong security with minimal overhead, whereas hybrid HE schemes selectively encrypt sensitive features to reduce the load. Additionally, model compression techniques, such as quantisation and knowledge distillation, lower resource usage while enhancing obfuscation. Additionally, adaptive participation enables weaker clients to perform local inference or validation, instead of complete training. These strategies ensure scalable and privacy-preserving FL across heterogeneous edge environments, as shown in **Figure 4**.

### 3.6 Balancing privacy and efficiency

Although FL offers inherent privacy benefits, decentralising data and implementing advanced privacy-preserving mechanisms often introduces trade-offs. Differential privacy can reduce the model accuracy by injecting noise. Secure aggregation may constrain scalability due to synchronisation, and encryption techniques, such as homomorphic encryption or secure multiparty computation, increase energy and latency costs. To address these challenges, emerging research advocates hybrid strategies, such as selective feature protection, lightweight cryptographic protocols, and layer-wise encryption, to optimise the balance between security and system efficiency. Ultimately, FL's privacy guarantees must be carefully calibrated against real-world performance needs, particularly in sectors with strict regulatory and resource constraints.

### 3.7 Legal and ethical implications in federated edge learning

FL, which keeps raw data decentralised, aligns with the privacy principles of global regulations, such as the GDPR and HIPAA. However, compliance extends beyond the architecture. Under the GDPR, FL systems must support informed user consent, enforce the right to be forgotten by isolating individual contributions, and implement anonymisation techniques to prevent data leakage through gradient updates. In healthcare, HIPAA compliance necessitates the implementation of audit trails, access controls, and the secure handling of Protected Health Information (PHI). Cross-cutting design strategies, such as privacy-by-design architectures, edge-aware consent management, and bounded differential privacy, ensure that FL systems not only protect data but also fulfil legal and ethical obligations in regulated domains.

#### *3.7.1 Future directions in privacy and security*

The evolving threat landscape in FL necessitates proactive and forward-looking security strategies, particularly given the emergence of quantum computing as a significant concern. Classical encryption techniques, such as RSA and ECC, commonly used in secure aggregation, are vulnerable to quantum attacks, most notably via Shor's algorithm, which can efficiently factor large integers. To address this issue, research is advancing in quantum-resistant cryptographic (PQC) methods tailored for constrained edge environments. Notable approaches include lattice-based schemes, such as Kyber and NTRU, and hash-based methods, which, although more computationally intensive, offer strong post-quantum security. Concurrently, AI-augmented threat detection is gaining traction, leveraging federated reinforcement learning to isolate malicious clients in real time, self-supervised anomaly detectors for adversarial updates, and graph neural networks (GNNs) to identify collusive behaviours across clients. These innovations pave the way for resilient, self-healing FL systems capable of defending against emerging zero-day and quantum threats.

## 4. Optimisation techniques for federated learning at the edge

FL at the edge faces unique optimisation challenges owing to constrained computational, communication, and energy resources. This section presents key strategies that improve the efficiency and scalability of FL in edge environments, organised under three themes: communication efficiency, computation and memory optimisation, and model generalisation. Mathematical concepts, comparative analyses, and relevant deployment implications are also discussed.

### 4.1 Communication efficiency optimisation

#### *4.1.1 Gradient compression*

Gradient compression reduces the amount of data transmitted during each FL communication round. A compressed version of the gradient vector $\tilde{g}_i$ is sent instead of the full gradient gig_igi, such that:

$\tilde{g}_i = Q(g_i)$,where Q(·) is a quantisation function.
Common methods include:

- *Top-k sparsification:* Send only the top-k gradient components.
- *Stochastic quantisation*: Each gradient component is quantised to a few bits (e.g. 2 bits).

These methods achieve a compression ratio $C_r$ given by:

$$C_r = \frac{\textit{Original gradient size}}{\textit{Compressed size}} \gg 1$$

*Trade-off*: Higher compression may reduce the model accuracy owing to information loss.

*4.1.2 Over-the-air aggregation*

Over-the-Air Computation (AirComp) leverages the superposition property of wireless channels to aggregate model updates during transmission:

$$\hat{G} = \sum_{i=1}^{N} h_i g_i + n$$

Where:

- $g_i$: Local model update from device,
- $h_i$: Channel gain,
- $n$: Gaussian noise term.

Channel inversion and power control algorithms are employed to mitigate aggregation noise. AirComp is particularly useful in dense networks because it reduces latency and bandwidth usage [10].

The principle behind over-the-air aggregation relies on analogue signal superposition, in which participating devices concurrently transmit their model updates over a shared wireless medium. Channel inversion is applied to ensure coherent aggregation at the receiver (e.g. edge aggregator). For a device with a complex channel gain $h_i$, the transmitted signal $x$ is pre-equalised as:

$$x_i = \frac{g_i}{h_i}$$

where $g_i$ is the local model update (or gradient vector). This ensures that the received signal at the aggregator becomes

$$y = \sum_{i=1}^{N} h_i x_i + n = \sum_{i=1}^{N} g_i + n$$

where $n$ is the additive white Gaussian noise (AWGN). Power control is critical in this context for maintaining the signal-to-noise ratio (SNR) under transmission power constraints. One common approach is to minimise the total transmission power.

$$min = \sum_{i=1}^{N} \left|\frac{g_i}{h_i}\right|^2 \text{ subject to } \left|\frac{g_i}{h_i}\right|^2 \leq P_{max}$$

where $P_{max}$ is the maximum transmission power of each edge device. Alternatively, devices can scale updates using a pre-determined gain $\alpha$ to maintain fairness:

$$x_i = \alpha * \frac{g_i}{h_i}, with\ \alpha = \frac{min}{i}\left(\sqrt{\frac{P_{max} * |h_i|^2}{||g_i||^2}}\right)$$

These techniques, when carefully coordinated, allow for efficient and accurate model aggregation while minimising bandwidth usage and preserving gradient integrity. However, this method is sensitive to channel estimation errors and requires time-synchronised transmission, which may limit its practicality in highly dynamic or heterogeneous environments.

## 4.2 Computation and memory efficiency

### *4.2.1 Model pruning*

Model pruning removes non-essential weights after or during training.

$$\omega' = \begin{cases} \omega_i, if\ |\omega_i| > \delta \\ 0, otherwise \end{cases}$$

where $\delta$ is a threshold. Techniques such as the Lottery Ticket Hypothesis (LTH) hypothesise the existence of sparse subnetworks ("winning tickets") that can be trained to achieve comparable accuracy.

*Impact*: Reduces model size and training time but may decrease accuracy.

### *4.2.2 Sparse training*

In sparse-to-sparse training, the model remains sparse throughout the training process. Training was performed only on the selected active weights. A sparse connectivity matrix $S \in \{0, 1\}^{n \times n}$ controls updates:

$$\frac{\partial \mathrm{L}}{\partial \omega_{\mathrm{i}}} = 0 \text{ if } \mathrm{S_{ij}} = 0$$

Sparse training can reduce memory usage by 80–90% in deep models [21].

## 4.3 Optimisation of learning dynamics

### *4.3.1 Adaptive learning rate and local updates*

Adaptive optimisation algorithms, such as Adam, Yogi, and FedNova, adjust the learning rate per parameter, thereby improving convergence stability. The local update at client iii after ttt steps is

$$\omega_i^{t+1} = \omega_i^t - \eta * \frac{m_t}{\sqrt{v_t} + \varepsilon}$$

where:

- $m_t$: First moment (mean),
- $v_t$: Second moment (uncentered variance).

*FedProx* further stabilises the updates using a proximal term to prevent divergence owing to data heterogeneity.

### 4.4 Knowledge distillation in FL

Knowledge distillation (KD) is employed when edge devices cannot host large models. A large teacher model TTT trains a compact student model SSS by minimising the divergence between their outputs:

$$L_{KD} = KL(S(x) \| T(x))$$

This enables the edge deployment of lightweight models while preserving the high-level performance learned from the entire model.

### 4.5 Comparative summary of optimisation techniques

**Table 6** highlights the comparative strengths and limitations of various FL optimisation strategies in edge computing scenarios. Techniques such as gradient compression and knowledge distillation reduce communication and model size, respectively, but at the cost of potential accuracy degradation or dependency on high-quality teacher models.

Sparse training and model pruning are suitable for constrained devices but require careful calibration. Over-the-air aggregation excels in dense networks but struggles under heterogeneous or noisy conditions. Asynchronous updates and adaptive optimisers enhance robustness but may slow down convergence. These trade-offs help guide optimisation decisions based on domain-specific priorities, such as latency, energy, and accuracy.

### 4.6 System-level optimisation framework

Efficient FL deployment at the edge requires a hierarchical optimisation framework that addresses device variability, connectivity, and data heterogeneity. The framework includes four coordinated layers: (1) Device Profiling, which monitors real-time metrics to guide adaptive participation and model scaling; (2) Model Allocation, which personalises and prunes models based on device capacity and local data; (3) Communication Control, which employs compression and asynchronous updates to minimise overhead; and (4) aggregation optimisation, which ensures robust, weighted model integration with resilience to faulty clients. The layered architecture, as illustrated in **Figure 5**, enables scalable, efficient, and secure federated learning tailored to edge environments.

In practical deployments, the multilayered FL optimisation framework operates adaptively. Device profiling (Layer 1) gathers metrics, such as battery and bandwidth,

| optimisation technique | Key objective | Trade-offs | Ideal edge scenario | Impact on accuracy | Impact on communication | Impact on computation |
|---|---|---|---|---|---|---|
| Gradient Compression | Reduce uplink communication | Slight drop in model accuracy due to lossy transmission | Low-bandwidth networks; IoT sensors | Moderate | High reduction | Minimal |
| Model Pruning | Reduce model size and cost | May underfit if pruning is aggressive | Devices with limited memory or CPU | Moderate | Moderate reduction | Moderate savings |
| Sparse Training | Improve memory and energy use | May slow convergence; requires structured sparsity | Resource-constrained devices (e.g. wearables) | Slight drop | Moderate reduction | High reduction |
| Over-the-Air Aggregation | Reduce communication latency | Sensitive to channel noise and synchronisation requirements | Dense sensor networks or UAV swarms | Low drop | Very high reduction | Low |
| Asynchronous Updates | Handle device dropout | Risk of model staleness; requires complex scheduling logic | Heterogeneous devices with intermittent connectivity | Moderate | Low reduction | Moderate |
| Knowledge Distillation | Model compression and privacy | Needs a high-quality teacher model; limited by dataset mismatch | Mobile phones with limited RAM, heterogeneous model needs | Moderate | High reduction | Moderate |
| Adaptive Optimisers (e.g. FedProx, FedNova) | Stability and convergence | Higher complexity and parameter tuning required | Cross-device FL with data heterogeneity | High | Neutral | Neutral |

**Table 6.**
*Federated learning optimisation techniques.*

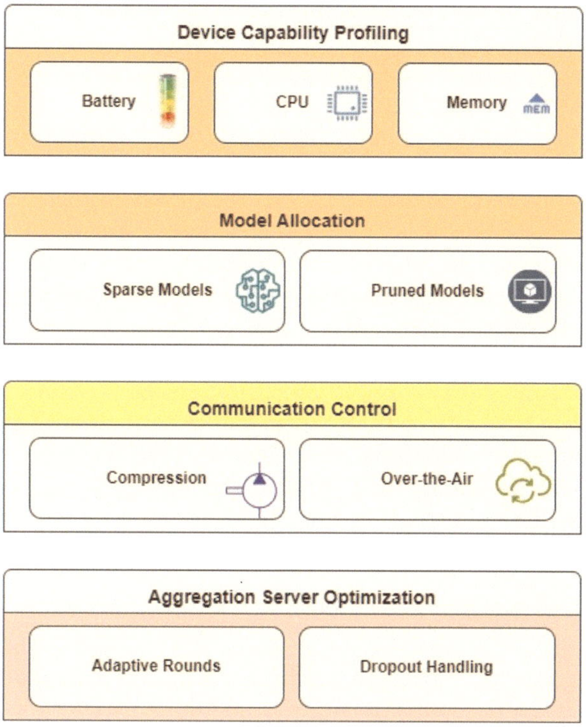


**Figure 5.**
*Multilayered optimisation framework for federated learning at the edge.*

which inform model allocation decisions (Layer 2), including the choice between full models and pruned variants. These inputs guide the communication strategies (Layer 3) by adjusting the compression or scheduling updates. Aggregation (Layer 4) then weights the client updates based on reliability and contribution quality. Real-world applications, such as smart agriculture and wearable healthcare, demonstrate the framework's flexibility, which enables resource-constrained devices to make meaningful contributions. Despite challenges such as synchronisation overhead or fairness in participation, solutions such as hybrid compression, adaptive scheduling, and blockchain auditing ensure the robustness and scalability of FL at the edge.

#### *4.6.1 Interplay between optimisation, privacy, and security in FL systems*

Optimisation strategies in FL often enhance communication and computation efficiency but may inadvertently weaken privacy and security. For example, gradient compression can disrupt the effectiveness of differential privacy (DP) depending on whether compression precedes or follows noise injection. Model pruning may expose dominant features, thereby increasing the vulnerability to inversion attacks. Although over-the-air aggregation is bandwidth-efficient, it risks gradient leakage without physical-layer encryption. Similarly, asynchronous updates can hinder anomaly detection and increase the risk of poisoning. Emerging solutions, such as privacy-aware compression and adversarial pruning, aim to balance these trade-offs. Thus, FL optimisation must adopt a holistic approach that considers utility, privacy, and security, particularly in resource-constrained edge deployments.

### 4.7 Emerging trends and future directions in FL optimisation

As FL evolves in edge environments, emerging optimisation techniques are enhancing its scalability, efficiency, and security. AI-driven strategies, such as reinforcement learning and meta-learning, enable dynamic adjustments in learning rates, client selection, and communication intervals, making FL more adaptable to fluctuating network conditions and device environments. Simultaneously, post-quantum cryptography, particularly lattice-based and code-based schemes, is being explored to secure model updates against future quantum threats, with ongoing work on lightweight versions suitable for edge devices. Neuromorphic and approximate computing are also being applied to reduce latency and energy demands, which are crucial for time-sensitive applications such as autonomous systems. Cross-layer co-optimisation frameworks are gaining momentum by jointly optimising the computation, communication, and system parameters. In contrast, federated analytics tools now incorporate fairness, trust, and carbon impact into their decision-making processes. These innovations, as illustrated in **Figure 6**, signal a shift toward intelligent, sustainable, and resilient FL architectures that are suitable for future edge AI deployments.

## 5. Experimental setup and evaluation methodology

To validate the feasibility and performance of FL in edge computing environments, we conducted a series of simulations using three popular FL algorithms: FedAvg, FedProx, and FedNova. Our goal was to assess their performance under real-world edge constraints, including non-IID data distribution, client dropouts, and limited communication bandwidth. The experimental setup and evaluation methodology were carefully designed to emulate realistic edge computing conditions and test the performance of FL in constrained environments. As shown in **Table 7**, two

**Figure 6.**
*Emerging optimisation techniques for federated learning at the edge.*

| Dataset | Task type | Clients | Partition basis | Data heterogeneity |
|---|---|---|---|---|
| FEMNIST | Handwritten character classification | 3400 | By user | High |
| Shakespeare | Next-character prediction | 660 | By actor/speaker role | High |

**Table 7.**
*Dataset and task design.*

| Component | Description |
|---|---|
| Framework | Flower (Python) |
| Host Machine | 16-core Intel Xeon CPU, 64 GB RAM |
| Simulated Clients | 1 GB RAM, low CPU quota, 20% dropout per round |

**Table 8.**
*Simulation environment.*

benchmark datasets, FEMNIST and Shakespeare, were selected to reflect high statistical heterogeneity, with data partitioned by users and speaker roles, respectively, across thousands of clients. This setup enabled the testing of non-IID behaviour in the client data distributions.

The simulation environment (see **Table 8**) was implemented using the Flower framework on a 16-core Intel Xeon server, with each client artificially constrained to 1 GB of RAM, minimal CPU resources, and a simulated 20% dropout rate to mirror real-world edge volatility. This allowed for a robust evaluation of dropout tolerance and communication resilience.

**Table 9** outlines the core hyperparameters: 100 global rounds, 5 local epochs, and a 10% client participation ratio per round. The experiments were repeated five times, and the mean results with 95% confidence intervals were reported to ensure statistical validity.

The evaluation metrics (summarised in **Table 10**) focused on four critical dimensions: model accuracy, convergence speed (i.e. the number of rounds required to achieve 80% accuracy), communication overhead (measured as the average megabyte (MB) per client per round), and dropout tolerance. These metrics collectively provide a comprehensive view of FL performance under edge-like constraints, with energy

| Parameter | Value |
|---|---|
| Global rounds | 100 |
| Local epochs | 5 |
| Learning rate | 0.01 |
| Batch size | 32 |
| Participation ratio | 10% per round |
| Dropout probability | 0.2 (randomised each round) |

**Table 9.**
*Hyperparameter settings.*

| Metric | Description |
|---|---|
| Model Accuracy | Final test accuracy of global model (%) |
| Convergence Speed | Rounds to reach 80% accuracy |
| Communication Overhead | Avg. MB per round per client |
| Dropout Tolerance | Avg. successful updates under 20% dropout |
| Future Work | Energy and latency measurements (not yet reported) |

**Table 10.**
*Evaluation metrics.*

and latency metrics designated for future inclusion. **Tables 7–10** define a reproducible, constraint-aware experimental framework that closely aligns with the realities of deploying FL in heterogeneous, resource-limited edge environments. Each experiment was repeated five times, and the mean values were reported with 95% confidence intervals.

## 5.1 Experimental setup and evaluation plan

To address the research objectives, this study adopts a mixed-methods approach that combines theoretical modelling, experimental simulations, and case-based analysis. Empirical evaluations were conducted to benchmark popular FL algorithms—FedAvg, FedProx, and FedNova—across critical performance metrics, including accuracy, convergence speed, communication overhead, and dropout tolerance. These evaluations reflect the practical challenges encountered in edge environments, such as limited bandwidth and intermittent connectivity issues. The results, detailed in Section 5, demonstrate that while FedProx achieves the highest accuracy (81.7%) and dropout tolerance (72%), FedNova exhibits superior communication efficiency and convergence. Complementing these findings, this chapter reviews architectural frameworks, privacy-preserving techniques, and optimisation strategies, including over-the-air aggregation, lottery ticket pruning, and model splitting, to assess the deployment of FL in real-world edge scenarios holistically. This multi-pronged methodology ensures analytical rigour and practical relevance. As shown in **Table 1**, FedProx demonstrates superior accuracy and robustness to device dropout, whereas FedNova offers improved communication efficiency and faster convergence, making it suitable for resource-constrained edge deployments.

**Figure 1** complements the tabular results by visually highlighting the performance trade-offs among the tested FL algorithms, facilitating an easier interpretation of their suitability for different edge scenarios.

To empirically evaluate the performance of FL strategies under edge computing constraints, we benchmarked three widely adopted algorithms—FedAvg, FedProx, and FedNova—across 100 communication rounds. As illustrated in **Figure 7**, all three algorithms demonstrated steady improvements in accuracy, with FedProx achieving the highest peak accuracy, followed by FedNova and FedAvg. However, the differences in accuracy progression were statistically insignificant, as confirmed by t-tests ($p > 0.3$ across all pairs), indicating similar model quality under non-IID data distributions. Conversely, the training loss trends shown in **Figure 8** reveal more pronounced distinctions. FedProx and FedNova achieved faster convergence and lower final loss values than FedAvg, reflecting better optimisation efficiency.

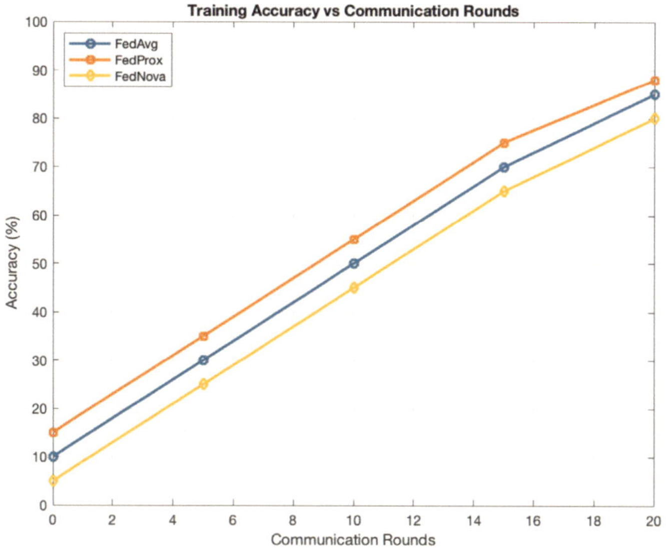


**Figure 7.**
*Accuracy trends over communication rounds.*

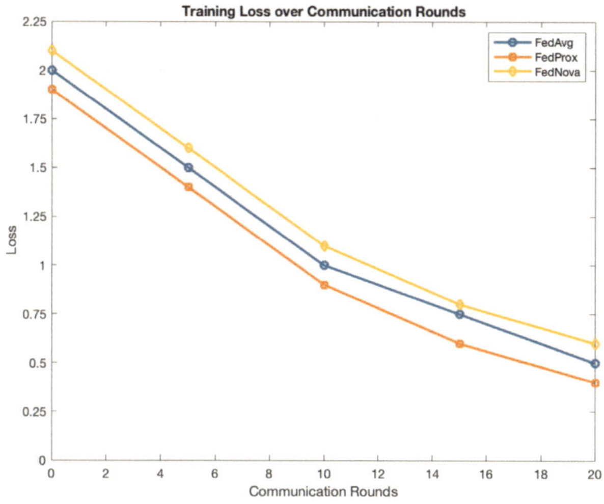


**Figure 8.**
*Loss trends over communication rounds.*

These observations were statistically validated, with significant differences in the final loss values between FedAvg and FedProx ($p = 0.0099$) and FedAvg and FedNova ($p = 0.0080$), as presented in **Table 11**. The superior performance of FedProx can be attributed to its proximal term, which mitigates client drift, whereas FedNova's normalised update mechanism enhances stability in heterogeneous environments. These findings underscore the importance of algorithm selection in FL deployments, particularly under bandwidth, energy, and heterogeneity constraints typical of edge computing scenarios.

In addition to benchmarking core FL strategies, we extended our experimental setup to simulate realistic edge constraints, such as client dropouts, network unreliability, and limited local resources. Client participation was randomised

| Comparison | t-statistic | p-value |
|---|---|---|
| FedAvg vs. FedProx (Accuracy) | 0.08349 | 0.93439 |
| FedAvg vs. FedNova (Accuracy) | −0.98937 | 0.3356 |
| FedProx vs. FedNova (Accuracy) | −1.01762 | 0.32234 |
| FedAvg vs. FedProx (Loss) | −2.88048 | 0.00996 |
| FedAvg vs. FedNova (Loss) | 2.97864 | 0.00805 |
| FedProx vs. FedNova (Loss) | 5.57256 | 0.00003 |

**Table 11.**
*T-Test results: Statistical comparison of accuracy and loss.*

| Constraint type | Simulation approach | Impact on FL performance |
|---|---|---|
| Device dropout | Random client unavailability (60–90% per round) | Affects convergence speed and final accuracy |
| Network unreliability | Delayed or failed update delivery | Reduces consistency and delays model updates |
| Compute limitations | Capped local training epochs or limited compute cycles | Slows convergence; may limit training depth |
| Data heterogeneity | Non-IID sampling across clients | Increases training instability and divergence |

**Table 12.**
*Simulated edge constraints In FL.*

between 60% and 90% per round to reflect intermittent availability, whereas local computation budgets were capped to simulate energy-constrained devices. We observed that both FedProx and FedNova maintained a more stable performance under these conditions than FedAvg, which was more sensitive to volatility. These constraints and their simulation strategies are summarised in **Table 12**, providing a reproducible foundation for future empirical studies on federated edge learning.

## 6. Applications and case studies of federated learning at the edge

FL is emerging as a transformative paradigm in edge computing, enabling the collaborative training of machine learning models while preserving user privacy and minimising communication overhead. This section presents an in-depth analysis of practical FL deployments across key sectors, including smart healthcare, smart mobility, industrial automation, and smart cities, while evaluating the system performance, privacy protection, and resource efficiency. The discussion aligns with the architectural and optimisation insights presented in the earlier sections and highlights the benchmarking outcomes and real-world implications.

### 6.1 Smart healthcare

FL is gaining widespread adoption in healthcare for tasks requiring privacy-preserving AI, such as diagnostics, predictive monitoring, and clinical decision-making

| Use case | Model type | Accuracy (AUC) | Privacy mechanism | Communication reduction |
|---|---|---|---|---|
| Arrhythmia Detection (Wearables) | CNN | 0.92 | DP + Local Training | 45% |
| Pneumonia Diagnosis (Hospitals) | CNN-RNN | 0.84 | SMC + Hierarchical FL | 37% |

**Table 13.**
*Federated learning use cases in smart healthcare [3, 4].*

support. A notable application involves wearable heart rate and ECG monitors collaborating via FL to predict cardiac abnormalities. Each device performs local training and contributes model updates to a shared global model without exposing raw patient data [3]. A real-world study across multiple hospitals, utilising the NIH chest radiograph dataset, implemented a federated CNN architecture. Despite data heterogeneity and device variability, the system achieved an average AUC of 0.84 across multiple diagnostic classes while meeting HIPAA compliance through differential privacy and secure multiparty computation. This is summarised in **Table 13**, which outlines the key FL applications in the healthcare domain, along with the performance metrics and privacy mechanisms.

## 6.2 Smart mobility and transportation

In intelligent transport systems (ITS), FL facilitates decentralised collaboration between vehicles, roadside units, and traffic sensors. For example, Tesla's Autopilot applies on-device learning where models are trained on individual cars and aggregated centrally. The author [22] evaluated FL-based traffic flow prediction in connected vehicles using asynchronous aggregation and over-the-air updates. The results showed a 43% reduction in training time, 31% savings in communication costs, and enhanced robustness to intermittent connectivity. **Table 14** presents two examples of FL deployments in smart mobility and their benefits.

## 6.3 Industrial internet of things (IIoT)

FL in IIoT enables distributed learning for tasks such as predictive maintenance, anomaly detection, and process optimisation in manufacturing. In a German automobile manufacturing plant, a federated fault detection system trained across heterogeneous edge devices, ranging from vibration sensors to PLCs, reduced unscheduled downtimes by 20%. Using a hierarchical FL setup, edge aggregators handle model updates locally before syncing with the cloud. This reduces latency and computation overhead while

| Use case | Optimisation used | RMSE | Bandwidth Savings | Privacy scheme |
|---|---|---|---|---|
| Traffic Flow Prediction | OTA + Sparse Aggregation | 0.87 | 31% | Local Model Sharing |
| Dynamic Route Optimisation | Pruned Model + Asynchronous | 0.85 | 28% | Blockchain-Enhanced FL |

**Table 14.**
*FL applications in smart mobility [10, 22].*

| use case | Accuracy | Privacy protocol | Efficiency gain | Deployment type |
|---|---|---|---|---|
| Vibration-Based Fault Detection | 0.89 | Hierarchical DP | 15% faster inference | Edge + Cloud Nodes |
| Energy Consumption Forecasting | 0.91 | Secure Aggregation | 17% comms reduction | Edge-Only Training |

**Table 15.**
*FL in industrial IoT applications.*

preserving operational confidentiality. **Table 15** compares two FL applications in IIoT in terms of their performance, efficiency, and deployment strategies.

## 6.4 Smart cities and public infrastructure

FL enhances city-scale systems, including environmental monitoring, surveillance and traffic control. In Barcelona's smart city initiative, FL enabled distributed air quality modelling using neighbourhood-level sensors. This approach minimises server bottlenecks and ensures compliance with the GDPR's privacy requirements. In Singapore, smart surveillance systems employ on-device training for facial and object recognition. FL preserves user anonymity while maintaining high detection accuracy and real-time responsiveness. **Table 16** illustrates the key performance outcomes of these FL deployments.

## 6.5 Performance analysis and benchmarking

Aggregating cross-sector performance data provides insights into FL's scalability and practical viability. A key consideration is balancing privacy, resource usage and model accuracy under edge constraints. **Figure 9** presents a benchmarking diagram that visualises FL's trade-offs across applications. **Figure 9** compares FL deployments across four major application domains—Smart Healthcare, Smart Mobility, IIoT, and Smart Cities—in terms of key parameters, including privacy requirements, latency sensitivity, communication efficiency, and model performance. This helps position FL strategies based on application-specific constraints, illustrating that while Smart Healthcare prioritises privacy and accuracy, mobility and IIoT focus more on low latency and communication efficiency.

FL demonstrates cross-domain adaptability by addressing sector-specific challenges related to privacy, latency, and communication. In healthcare and surveillance, privacy preservation is paramount, whereas IIoT and mobility applications emphasise real-time responsiveness and fault resilience. **Figure 10** benchmarks the FL performance across Smart Healthcare, Smart Mobility, Industrial IoT (IIoT), and Smart Cities along four axes: privacy requirement, latency sensitivity, communication efficiency, and model performance. Smart Healthcare scores are highest in privacy and accuracy demands, whereas Smart Mobility leads in latency and communication needs

| Application | Model accuracy | Communication overhead | Compliance |
|---|---|---|---|
| Air Quality Prediction | 0.85 R^2 | 30% reduced | GDPR-Compliant |
| Public Surveillance | 0.90 F1-score | 50% reduced | On-device + DP |

**Table 16.**
*FL in smart city and public infrastructure.*

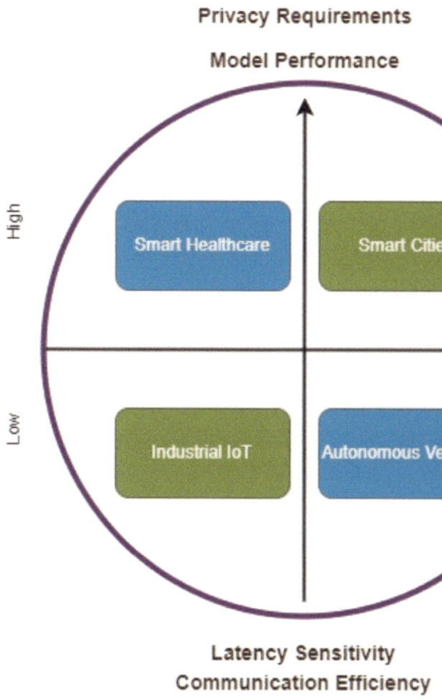


**Figure 9.**
*FL's trade-offs across applications.*

due to its real-time operational context. The IIoT focuses on communication and reliability, and Smart Cities present balanced requirements across all dimensions. These benchmarks guide the selection of FL strategies, including privacy-centric designs for healthcare, low-latency aggregation for mobility, and scalable, adaptive frameworks for smart cities. Looking ahead, the integration of personalised FL, quantum-resilient cryptography, and intelligent scheduling mechanisms will further strengthen FL's deployment in sensitive and resource-constrained environments.

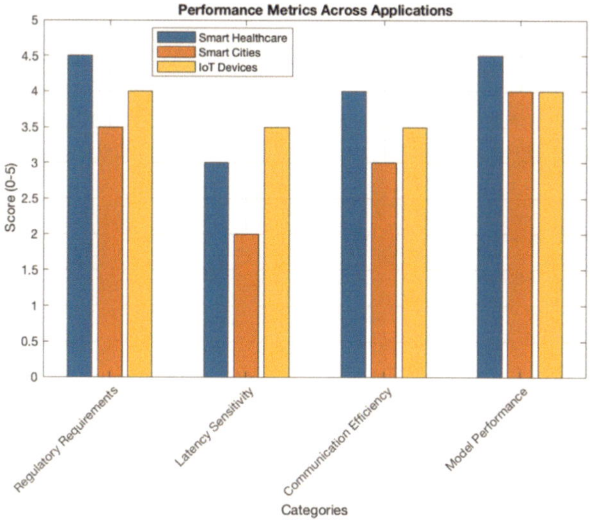


**Figure 10.**
*Benchmarking FL applications across sectors.*

## 7. Next-generation strategies for edge-centric FL

### 7.1 Personalisation in federated edge learning

Personalisation is a key response to the challenge of non-identically distributed (non-IID) data in FL at the edge, where client distributions vary due to localised usage patterns. Standard global models often underperform in such settings. Simple local fine-tuning enables clients to adapt the global model to their specific data; however, it also risks overfitting. More structured approaches, such as federated personalisation layers (FedPer), separate shared and local layers within the network, enabling both collaboration and individuality. Clustered FL techniques (e.g. FedCluster) segments clients with similar data into groups to support targeted model updates, which is especially useful in applications such as personalised healthcare.

Meta-learning approaches (such as FedMeta) aim for generalisable model initialisations that can be quickly adapted per client with minimal data. These personalisation strategies enhance the local model performance, with varying trade-offs in complexity and scalability. **Table 17** summarises these techniques, highlighting their strengths and deployment considerations in edge environments.

### 7.2 Incentive mechanisms in federated edge learning

Incentivising participation inFL at the edge is essential because of the voluntary and resource-constrained nature of client devices. Without adequate motivation, devices may underperform, submit low-quality updates, or become disengaged. Several incentive models have been proposed to address this issue. Reputation-based systems reward clients with strong historical performance but face challenges in dynamic environments and vulnerability to collusion [8]. Game-theoretic approaches, such as those using Shapley value estimations, offer fair payoff structures but often entail high computational overhead [2]. Blockchain-enabled mechanisms utilise smart contracts for transparent reward distribution, thereby enhancing trust, but at the expense of increased latency and resource intensity [6].

Additionally, auction-based strategies dynamically select clients based on utility-driven bids, though these require mechanisms to prevent strategic manipulation [8]. Together, these strategies highlight the balance between fairness, computational

| Technique | Description | Pros | Limitations |
|---|---|---|---|
| Fine-tuning | Post-FL local training | Simple, low overhead | Risk of overfitting, lacks coordination |
| FedPer | Personal and shared layers in NN | Efficient for structured heterogeneity | Requires shared model architecture |
| FedCluster | Cluster clients based on data similarity | Boosts accuracy for skewed distributions | Needs an effective clustering strategy |
| Meta-FL (FedMeta) | Learns adaptable initialisations | Fast convergence on client data | Higher training complexity |

**Table 17.**
*Summary of personalisation techniques in federated learning [2, 4, 5].*

| Incentive type | Description | Strengths | Limitations |
|---|---|---|---|
| Reputation-based | Score clients using historical performance | Encourages consistent participation | Susceptible to manipulation, needs monitoring |
| Game-theoretic models | Allocate rewards via utility/payoff functions | Fairness grounded in formal theory | High computational overhead |
| Blockchain-integrated | Use smart contracts for transparent incentives | Tamper-proof, autonomous compensation | High latency and energy costs |
| Auction-based selection | Clients bid for participation based on capacity | Scalable, cost-optimised client selection | Vulnerable to strategic bidding |

**Table 18.**
*Comparative overview of incentive mechanisms in federated edge learning.*

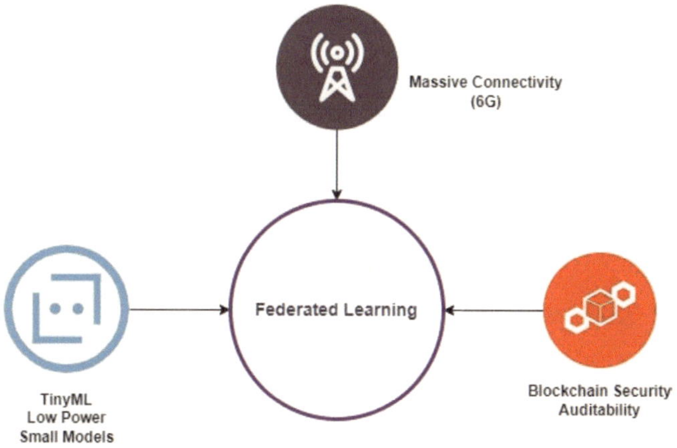


**Figure 11.**
*A conceptual diagram showing how FL integrates with 6G, blockchain, and TinyML.*

feasibility, and trust in sustaining edge FL ecosystems. The strengths and limitations of these approaches are summarised in **Table 18**.

## 7.3 Integration with next-generation technologies

The integration of 6G, blockchain, and TinyML can significantly enhance the scalability and robustness of FL at the edge. Sixth-generation (6G) networks offer ultra-reliable low-latency communication and massive connectivity, enabling real-time aggregation and consistent client participation in dynamic edge scenarios [8]. Blockchain adds decentralised trust and auditability, ensuring secure aggregation, transparent participation, and smart contract-based incentives [6]. Meanwhile, TinyML facilitates local learning on ultra-low-power devices, supporting privacy-preserving and cloud-independent FL, although it requires compressed models and energy-efficient protocols [9]. These technologies collectively form the foundation for secure, low-latency, and scalable FL systems, as illustrated in **Figure 11**.

## 8. Challenges and future directions

FL at the edge presents transformative opportunities for privacy-preserving and decentralised intelligence; however, several open challenges and research frontiers remain. This section builds on the themes established throughout the chapter and outlines coherent directions for researchers and practitioners seeking to advance the state of the art.

### 8.1 Personalisation and statistical heterogeneity

A persistent issue in FL is non-identically distributed (non-IID) data across edge nodes, leading to poor generalisation of the global model. Personalisation techniques, such as meta-learning, multitask learning, and local fine-tuning, are critical for bridging this gap. Future research should investigate how these approaches can dynamically adapt to varying client contexts, data sparsity, and domain shifts without significantly increasing the communication or computation overhead.

### 8.2 Incentive mechanisms for sustainable participation

FL at scale depends on voluntary and consistent participation by edge clients. However, motivating heterogeneous device owners to engage remains a challenge. Blockchain-based incentive mechanisms, token economics, and reputation systems show promise; however, their implementation must account for fairness, energy efficiency, and resistance to gaming. Researchers should focus on transparent, low-overhead, equitable, and verifiable incentive mechanisms.

### 8.3 Integrating federated learning with blockchain

The combination of FL and blockchain enhances trust, auditability, and secure collaborations. Smart contracts can automate model update validation, rewards, and governance processes. However, the integration of blockchain into FL introduces latency, consensus costs, and storage overhead. Research is required on lightweight blockchain protocols tailored to FL, off-chain computation strategies, and privacy-preserving consensus mechanisms that scale across diverse edge devices.

### 8.4 Synergy with TinyML

TinyML enables ML inference on ultra-low-power devices, making it a natural partner for FL in extreme-edge settings. However, training models collaboratively on such devices remains an open challenge because of memory, computing, and power limitations. Techniques such as gradient sparsification, quantised updates, and federated distillation should be extended and optimised for microcontroller-class hardware. The development of toolkits that bridge the FL and TinyML ecosystems will be instrumental.

### 8.5 Convergence with 6G technologies

The imminent rollout of 6G networks, which provide ultra-reliable low-latency communication (URLLC), massive device connectivity, and integrated AI, will be pivotal for the scalability of FL. Future studies should explore how FL frameworks can leverage 6G innovations, such as network slicing, intelligent reflecting surfaces (IRS), and semantic communication, to improve reliability and efficiency under dynamic edge conditions.

### 8.6 Robustness against emerging threats

Security and privacy remain the top concerns in FL. Model poisoning, backdoor attacks, and inference leakage through gradients are significant threats. Countermeasures such as anomaly detection, Byzantine-resilient aggregation, and secure multiparty computation require further refinement, particularly for low-power devices. Research should also explore quantum-resilient cryptography and lightweight adaptive defence mechanisms that are suitable for dynamic and adversarial edge environments.

### 8.7 Standardisation and benchmarking

Currently, the evaluation of FL frameworks across application domains lacks standardisation, which impedes reproducibility and comparative analysis. Establishing benchmarks that account for device heterogeneity, network variability, and data distribution will support rigorous evaluation and validation. Collaborative efforts are required to develop open FL testbeds that reflect real-world constraints in healthcare, mobility, and industrial systems.

## 9. Conclusion

This chapter provides a comprehensive examination of FL at the edge, including its motivations, system architectures, optimisation strategies, privacy and security safeguards, and real-world applications. Through theoretical modelling, comparative tables, and detailed benchmarking, we outline how FL can be tailored to meet the nuanced demands of edge computing environments. Although FL promises scalable and privacy-aware intelligence, it is not without challenges. Heterogeneity, limited resources, communication bottlenecks, and security risks are ongoing barriers. As this chapter emphasises, addressing these issues requires a convergence of innovations in communication protocols, distributed optimisation, hardware-aware algorithms, and privacy-preserving techniques.

Looking ahead, the intersection of FL with technologies such as blockchain, 6G, and TinyML will redefine the landscape of intelligent edge systems. By establishing robust incentive mechanisms, aligning with regulatory frameworks, and building adaptable architectures, researchers and practitioners can drive the evolution of FL into a secure, fair, and high-performance paradigm. As FL matures, it will serve as the cornerstone of the architecture for responsible AI, enabling ubiquitous data-driven decision-making.

## Author details

Kofi Sarpong Adu-Manu[1*], Prince Samuel Kyeremanteng[1], Prince Ofori[1], Charles Adjetey[2], Pachomius Kwaku Lawson[1] and Eugene Cobbah[1]

1 Department of Computer Science, University of Ghana, Accra, Ghana

2 Department of Computer Science and Information Systems, Ashesi University, Accra, Ghana

*Address all correspondence to: ksadu-manu@ug.edu.gh

## References

[1] Xia Q, Ye W, Tao Z, Wu J, Li K. A survey of federated learning for edge computing: Research problems and solutions. High-Confidence Computing. 2021;**1**(1):100001. DOI: 10.1016/j.hcc.2021.100001

[2] Costan A, Antoniu G, Bougé L. Enabling federated learning across the computing continuum: Systems, challenges and future directions. Future Generation Computer Systems. 2024;**150**:112-127. DOI: 10.1016/j.future.2023.08.012

[3] Tang X, Guo S, Liu J. An efficient and dynamic privacy-preserving federated learning system for edge computing. IEEE Transactions on Information Forensics and Security. 2024;**19**:1563-1576. DOI: 10.1109/TIFS.2023.3334567

[4] Gawalkar S. Federated learning for privacy-preserving AI in edge and IoT devices. International Scientific Journal of Engineering and Management. 2025;**4**(2):1-10. [Online]. Available from: https://isjem.com

[5] Li J, Yan H, Huang T. Efficient federated learning with enhanced privacy via lottery ticket pruning in edge computing. IEEE Transactions on Mobile Computing. 2023;**22**(5):2801-2814. DOI: 10.1109/TMC.2022.3156789

[6] Niyato FIHV, Niyato D, Wang P, Han H. Federated learning meets blockchain in edge computing: Opportunities and challenges. IEEE Internet of Things Journal. 2021;**8**(12):9725-9740. DOI: 10.1109/JIOT.2021.3068791

[7] Xiong N, Liu RW, Liang M, Wu Y. LightFed: An efficient and secure federated edge learning system on model splitting. IEEE Transactions on Parallel and Distributed Systems. 2021;**32**(11):2701-2714. DOI: 10.1109/TPDS.2021.3070832

[8] Zhang Y, Zhou Y, Liu X. Decentralized edge intelligence: A dynamic resource allocation framework for hierarchical federated learning. IEEE Transactions on Parallel and Distributed Systems. 2022;**33**(3):536-549. DOI: 10.1109/TPDS.2021.3097945

[9] Ghader M, Alahi A, Aberer K. Enabling privacy-preserving edge AI: Federated learning enhanced with forward-forward algorithm. In: 2024 IEEE International Conference on Omni-layer Intelligent Systems (COINS). Piscataway, NJ, USA: IEEE; 2024. pp. 1-8. DOI: 10.1109/COINS61574.2024.10601345

[10] Cui S, Yang W, Zhang Z. An overview on over-the-air federated edge learning. IEEE Wireless Communications. 2022;**29**(4):88-95. DOI: 10.1109/MWC.001.2100523

[11] Yu S, Chen X, Zhou Z. CEFL: Online admission control, data scheduling, and accuracy tuning for cost-efficient federated learning across edge nodes. IEEE Internet of Things Journal. 2020;**7**(10):9341-9356. DOI: 10.1109/JIOT.2020.2987890

[12] Tian J, Zhang Y, Li C. Leveraging federated learning and edge computing for recommendation systems within cloud computing networks. IEEE Internet of Things Journal. 2024;**11**(7):12345-12358. DOI: 10.1109/JIOT.2023.3312345

[13] TensorFlow Federated Team. TensorFlow Federated Documentation. Mountain View, CA, USA: Google; 2024. [Online]. Available from: https://www.tensorflow.org/federated

[14] Beutel D, Topal T, Qiu X, et al. Flower: A Friendly Federated Learning Framework. Flower Labs; 2024. [Online]. Available from: https://flower.dev/docs

[15] Ryffel T, Trask A, et al. PySyft: Encrypted, Privacy-Preserving Machine Learning. OpenMined; 2024. [Online]. Available from: https://www.pysyft.org

[16] Hitaj B, Ateniese G, Perez-Cruz F. Deep models under the GAN: Information leakage from collaborative deep learning. In: Proceedings of the 2017 ACM SIGSAC Conference on Computer and Communications Security. New York, NY, USA: ACM; 2017. pp. 603-618. DOI: 10.1145/3133956.3134015

[17] Bagdasaryan E, Veit A, Hua Y, Estrin D, Shmatikov V. How to backdoor federated learning. In: Proceedings of the 23rd International Conference on Artificial Intelligence and Statistics. Vol. 108. PMLR; 2020. pp. 2938-2948. [Online]. Available from: https://proceedings.mlr.press/v108/bagdasaryan20a.html

[18] Geyer RC, Klein T, Nabi M. Differentially private federated learning: A client level perspective. arXiv preprint arXiv:1712.07557. Ithaca, NY, USA: arXiv; 2017. [Online]. Available from: https://arxiv.org/abs/1712.07557

[19] Thakurta A, Smith A, Thakurta A. Practical locally private heavy hitters. In: Proceedings of the 2017 ACM Symposium on Principles of Database Systems. New York, NY, USA: ACM; 2017. pp. 273-300. DOI: 10.1145/3034786.3056120

[20] Bonawitz K, Ivanov V, Kreuter B, Marcedone A, McMahan HB, Patel S, et al. Practical secure aggregation for privacy-preserving machine learning. In: Proceedings of the 2017 ACM SIGSAC Conference on Computer and Communications Security. New York, NY, USA: ACM; 2017. pp. 117-135. DOI: 10.1145/3133956.3133982

[21] Evci U, Gale T, Menick J, Castro PS, Elsen E. Rigging the lottery: Making all tickets winners. In: Proceedings of the 37th International Conference on Machine Learning (ICML). Vol. 119. PMLR; 2020. pp. 2943-2953. [Online]. Available from: https://proceedings.mlr.press/v119/evci20a.html

[22] Lin W, Xu S, Liu L. Accelerating federated learning over reliability-agnostic clients in mobile edge computing systems. IEEE Transactions on Parallel and Distributed Systems. 2020;**31**(4):978-991. DOI: 10.1109/TPDS.2019.2955278

Chapter 2

# Extreme Multistability in a Dynamic System with Infinitely Many 2D Hidden Attractors

*Lizbeth Vargas-Cabrera, Olga G. Félix-Beltrán, Jesus Manuel Munoz-Pacheco and Viet-Thanh Pham*

## Abstract

Extreme multistability can be understood as a dynamical behavior in which new attractors arise from infinitesimal variations in initial conditions. In this chapter, we introduce a novel continuous-time dynamical system governed by periodic signals as the main nonlinearities that converges to 2D infinitely many chaotic attractors in the phase space. Notably, the chaotic system has no stationary equilibrium points. In addition, a single parameter controls the class of a hidden attractor, that is, from an infinite mesh of equilibria to no equilibrium points. Theoretical and numerical experiments, including equilibrium point analysis and Poincaré maps, reveal the striking properties of the chaotic system. The resulting outcomes open up possibilities for application in chaos-based data encryption.

**Keywords:** chaotic system, infinitely many attractors, extreme multistability, Poincaré maps, hidden attractors

## 1. Introduction

Since Lorenz discovered an atmospheric dynamical model that generates a chaotic attractor [1], also known as the butterfly effect, the theory of chaotic systems has attracted considerable interest from the scientific community. Henceforth, several chaotic systems modeled by ordinary differential equations have been studied. They have been classified from many viewpoints as follows:

- Autonomous and non-autonomous chaotic systems. This is related to the nature of the external source. Time-varying external sources give rise to non-autonomous systems [2], whereas in autonomous systems, the equations of motion do not explicitly depend on time [3].

- Continuous and discrete chaotic systems. This means that if the chaotic system is defined in continuous time or discrete time, such as flows [4] and maps [5], respectively.

- Integer-order and fractional-order chaotic systems. When fractional-order derivatives describe the left-hand side of the dynamical system, the resulting system is a fractional-order one [6]. Otherwise, it is a classical integer-order system [7].

- Self-excited and hidden attractors. According to whether the chaotic attractors are found through the equilibrium points or not [8].

For all previous families of chaotic systems, it is well known that if there is at least one positive Lyapunov exponent, the system is considered chaotic [9]. Another way to determine the existence of chaos is through the Sil'nikov criterion [10], which involves calculating the equilibrium points of the given system and then using homoclinic or heteroclinic orbits connecting these equilibrium points to detect the presence of chaos. However, as we can note, the Sil'nikov criterion cannot be applied to dynamical systems without equilibrium points.

When Leonov and Kutnesov published the seminal papers about hidden phenomena in dynamical systems [11, 12], an attractor is called hidden if its basin of attraction does not intersect any neighborhood of equilibria [13]. It means that the attractor cannot be found by starting integration near a fixed point and even when the basin of attraction is relatively narrow, which requires special initial conditions. Also, the attractors from dynamical systems without equilibrium points, with curves and surfaces of equilibrium, or with only stable equilibria, are hidden attractors [14]. It is well known that hidden attractors have been discovered in several dynamical systems [8, 14–16], such as in Chua's circuit, Lorenz-like systems, and piecewise nonlinear systems. From an engineering perspective, hidden attractors can facilitate the analysis and comprehension of unexpected responses in dynamical systems [17, 18].

In this paper, we propose a new dynamical system dominated by sinusoidal nonlinearities. An essential feature of this dynamical system is that it generates an infinite number of hidden attractors, that is, extreme multistability with the modification of a single parameter. We can move from a chaotic system with an infinite number of equilibrium points to a chaotic system with no equilibrium points. Extreme multistability results in distinct chaotic attractors within a given nonlinear dynamical system, even for the same set of parameters. Because the proposed chaotic system contains no unnecessary terms and its system parameters have the minimum number of digits, it satisfies the Sprott criterion for elegant dynamical systems.

The chapter is organized as follows. Section 2 introduces the proposed extreme multistable chaotic system. Stability analysis is also performed. Section 3 presents numerical results demonstrating the extreme multistability and the infinitely many 2D chaotic attractors. Section 4 gives the conclusion and future work.

## 2. Proposed chaotic system and its nonlinear dynamics

Inspired by the work in Ref. [8], we propose a novel dynamical system, whose key difference is adding trigonometric functions to control the $x$ and $y$ variables as follows:

$$\dot{x} = zP\sin y + \sin x(P\sin y - Q), \tag{1}$$

$$\dot{y} = 1 - R\sin|x|, \tag{2}$$

$$\dot{z} = -\sin xP\sin y - z, \tag{3}$$

where $x, y, z \in \mathbb{R}$ are the system variables and $P$, $Q$, and $R$ are real parameters, with $\sin(\cdot)$ and $|\cdot|$ as the nonlinearities. The next step is to compute the equilibrium points of the proposed chaotic system. In dynamical systems, we define an equilibrium point as the values of variables at which the right-hand side function equals zero while the derivative is also zero, that is, $f(w(t), t) = 0$, with $w(t) = (x, y, z)$. To help determine the chaos phenomenon, it is necessary to calculate and classify the system's equilibrium points according to their stability. It is essential to note that the number of equilibrium points for an autonomous nonlinear dynamical system, such as the one in Eqs. (1)-(3), is not determined by the number of differential equations, unlike in the case of a linear system. Thus, the nonlinear dynamical system may have an indeterminate number of equilibrium points, ranging from extreme cases with no equilibrium points to an infinite number. Depending on the stability of such equilibria, it opens the door to hidden attractors. By equating the chaotic system to zero, we can determine the equilibrium points as follows:

$$0 = zP\sin y + \sin x(P\sin y - Q), \tag{4}$$

$$0 = 1 - R\sin|x|, \tag{5}$$

$$0 = -\sin xP\sin y - z. \tag{6}$$

Due to the absolute value function, we consider a first case with $x \geq 0$. Thus, from Eq. (5), we have

$$x = \arcsin(1/R) + n\pi. \tag{7}$$

Now, solving for $P\sin y$ in Eq. (6), we obtain

$$P\sin y = -\frac{z}{\sin x}. \tag{8}$$

Substituting Eq. (8) into Eq. (4), we have

$$\begin{aligned} z\left(-\frac{z}{\sin x}\right) + \sin x\left(-\frac{z}{\sin x} - Q\right) = 0, \\ \frac{z^2}{\sin x} + z + Q\sin x = 0. \end{aligned} \tag{9}$$

Due to $\sin x = 1/R$, it produces a quadratic equation in $z$. Therefore, we can use the well-known solution for this kind of equation, yielding

$$z_{1,2} = -\frac{1}{2R} \pm \frac{\sqrt{1-4Q}}{2R}. \tag{10}$$

We observe that if the parameter $Q$ in the radicand is lower than a determined value, that is, $Q \leq 0.25$, Eq. (10) has many solutions due to the periodicity of the trigonometric functions $\sin x$ and $\sin y$. In this manner, we can conclude that the chaotic system has infinitely many equilibrium points propagated over the $x - z$ phase plane [15]. On the contrary, if $Q > 0.25$, Eq. (10) has no real solutions, resulting in a chaotic system belonging to the family of hidden attractors with no equilibrium points [19].

In addition, another meaningful metric in dynamical systems is the divergence given by

$$\nabla V = \frac{\partial \dot{x}}{\partial x} + \frac{\partial \dot{y}}{\partial y} + \frac{\partial \dot{z}}{\partial z}, \tag{11}$$

which measures the instantaneous rate of volume change in the phase space. Here, $\nabla$ is the vector differential operator, and $\nabla V \in \mathbb{R}$ defines the divergence of the vector field. For chaotic systems, it is expected that $\nabla V < 0$. It indicates that although nearby trajectories diverge locally, the total volume is confined in a finite phase space, that is, the attractor. In our case, the divergence of the flow of the proposed chaotic system is

$$\nabla V = \cos x(P \sin y - Q) - 1, \tag{12}$$

As we can see, the divergence depends not only on the system parameters $(P, Q, R)$ but also on the system variables $x$ and $y$. In this manner, $\nabla V$ changes as $x$ and $y$ evolve in time, and therefore, it is neither constant nor smaller than zero. In such cases, we also need to ensure that the average divergence is negative, confirming bounded chaos. This assumption is numerically demonstrated by computing the average of $\nabla V$ as depicted in **Figure 1**. In both cases, $Q = -1$ and $Q = 0.65$, and the divergence is negative as time approaches infinity, which guarantees the proposed chaotic systems may have a chaotic attractor.

Once the equilibrium points are computed, the next step is to determine the stability. The stability analysis examines the behavior of the initial conditions in the neighborhood of each equilibrium point. Therefore, the nature of the equilibrium points is essentially determined by the eigenvalues of the chaotic system, which are obtained by solving the characteristic equation of the Jacobian matrix, and can be classified according to Sprott classification [20]. The Jacobian matrix of the underlying chaotic system is given as

$$J = \begin{pmatrix} \cos x(P \sin y - Q) & P \cos y(z + \sin x) & 0 \\ -R \cos x & 0 & 0 \\ -\cos x P \sin y & -\sin x P \cos y & -1 \end{pmatrix}, \tag{13}$$

where $J \in \mathbb{R}^{3\times 3}$ is a matrix of appropriate dimensions. It is well known that establishing the dissipativity property is a complex task.

Finally, without loss of generality, similar results for the Jacobian matrix $J$ can be derived for the instance when $|x| < 0$. Based on the previous discussion, the stability analysis is divided into two scenarios as shown in the following subsections.

### 2.1 Hidden 2D mesh of chaotic attractors with an infinite number of equilibria

In this case, we consider $Q = -1$, $P = 7$, and $R = 5$. Since $Q \leq 0.25$, we can find the equilibrium points using a graphical approach as follows. First, we obtain a

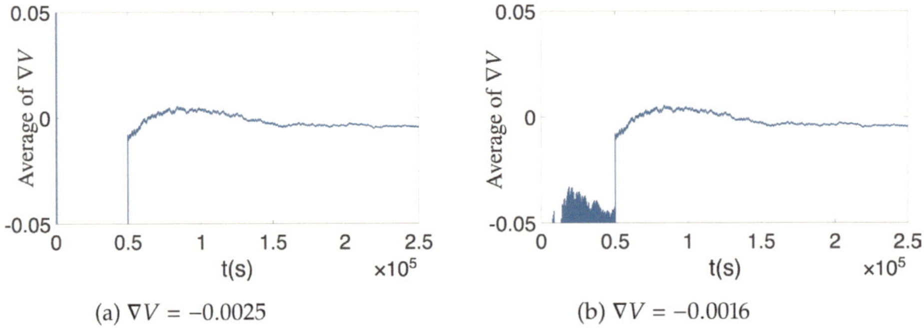


**Figure 1.**
*Mean value of divergence $\nabla V$ for the following cases. (a) Infinite number of equilibria ($Q = -1$) and (b) no equilibrium points ($Q = 0.65$).*

pair of functions $f_1(z, y)$ and $f_2(z, y)$. The function $f_1(z, y)$, derived from Eq. (6), has the form of

$$z = -\frac{P}{R}\sin y, \tag{14}$$

while the second function $f_2(z, y)$ obtained by Eq. (4) is given by

$$z = -\frac{1}{R} + \frac{Q}{RP}\csc y. \tag{15}$$

Then, when both functions $f_1$ and $f_2$ intersect, we obtain the equilibrium point. **Figure 2a** shows the equilibrium points of the proposed chaotic system. By plotting the functions $f_1$ and $f_2$ in the interval $y = (-4, 4)$, we can find the intersection points between both functions. Such crossing points provide explicit values for the infinite equilibrium points of the chaotic system. For instance, when the system parameters are $Q = -1$, $P$=7, and $R$4=5, we obtain $EP_1$=(0.20,0.21,-0.29) and $EP_2$=(−0.20,-0.06,0.09). It is worth noting that, as the periodic signal evolves to $t \to \infty$, the number of equilibrium points does.

As a result, the equilibria are infinitely distributed in a 2D mesh on the $x-y$ phase plane. Depending on their stability, it opens the possibility of generating hidden attractors whose localization depends on the initial conditions. This may produce infinitely many hidden attractors. In particular, the equilibrium points $EP = (x^*, y^*, z^*)$ when $|x| \geq 0$ and $|x| < 0$ are expressed, respectively, as

$$EP_1 = \left(\arcsin(1/R) \pm n\pi,\ -\arcsin\frac{\sqrt{1-4Q}-1}{2P} \pm n\pi,\ -\frac{1}{2R} + \frac{\sqrt{1-4Q}}{2R}\right), \tag{16}$$

$$EP_2 = \left(\arcsin(1/R) \pm n\pi,\ \arcsin\frac{\sqrt{1-4Q}+1}{2P} \pm n\pi,\ -\frac{1}{2R} - \frac{\sqrt{1-4Q}}{2R}\right), \tag{17}$$

$$EP_3 = \left(\arcsin(-1/R) \pm n\pi,\ \arcsin\frac{\sqrt{1-4Q}+1}{2P} \pm n\pi, \frac{1}{2R} + \frac{\sqrt{1-4Q}}{2R}\right), \tag{18}$$

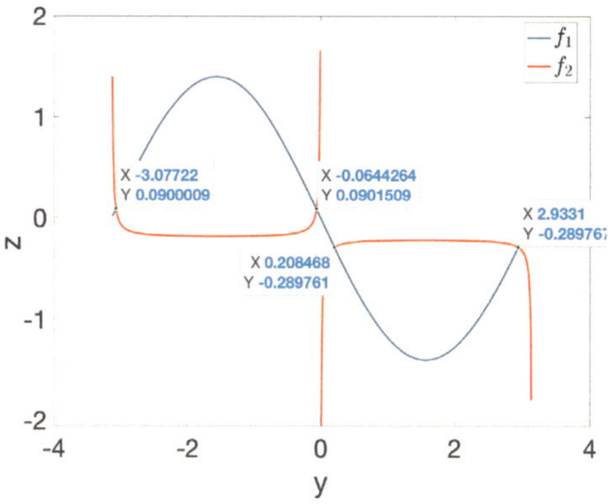


(a) $Q = -1$

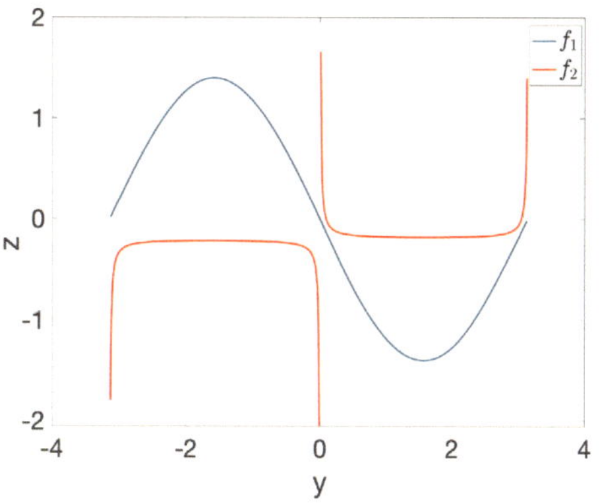


(b) $Q = 0.65$

**Figure 2.**
*Graphical determination of the equilibrium points in the proposed chaotic system by plotting the functions $f_1$: $z = -P/R \sin y$ and $f_2$: $z = -1/R + (Q/RP) \csc y$ in the interval $y=(-4,4)$ for the cases (a) with an infinite number of equilibria and (b) without equilibrium points.*

$$EP_4 = \left(\arcsin(-1/R) \pm n\pi, -\arcsin\frac{\sqrt{1-4Q}-1}{2P} \pm n\pi, \frac{1}{2R} - \frac{\sqrt{1-4Q}}{2R}\right), \quad (19)$$

with $EP_1$, $EP_2$, $EP_3$, and $EP_4$ being the equilibrium points of the proposed chaotic system and $n$ meaning the number of periods of function $\sin(\cdot)$.

### 2.2 Hidden infinity 2D mesh of chaotic attractors without equilibrium points

We now consider the scenario with $Q = 0.65$, $P = 7$, and $R = 5$. Since $Q > 0.25$, the equilibrium points cannot be found using traditional methods. For example, the radicand in Eq. (10) becomes negative for $Q > 0.25$. Then, the solutions $z_1$ and $z_2$ are purely imaginary. The non-existence of equilibrium points is also verified graphically using the functions $f_1$ and $f_2$ in Eqs. (12) and (13) as sketched in **Figure 2b**. By plotting both functions in the interval $y=(-4,4)$, it can be observed that both functions never intersect, and therefore, there are no real solutions for the variable $z$. This means that stability cannot be analyzed using the standard fixed-point theory, which requires solutions in the real number domain.

Definition 1 **(hidden attractor)**. An attractor is called hidden if it satisfies the following assumptions [11]:

1. Its base of attraction does not intersect with any open neighborhood of an equilibrium point.

2. The number of equilibrium points of the dynamical system is infinite.

3. All equilibrium points of the dynamical system are stable, that is, the real part of the eigenvalues is non-positive and different from zero.

4. It has no equilibrium points.

It is well known that chaotic systems with hidden attractors can exhibit interesting nonlinear dynamics, such as bistability, multistability, and extreme multistability.

Definition 2 **(multistability)**. Multistability refers to the coexistence of attractors under the same system parameters, but with different initial conditions [14].

Definition 3 **(extreme multistability)**. A chaotic system converges to extreme multistability if its response leads to entirely different qualitative behavior for the same parameter values with minimal variation in its initial conditions [21]. That is, extreme multistability is a special type of multistability related to infinitely many attractors; therefore, new attractors are generated based on the tiniest variations in the initial conditions, and even in the observation time.

## 3. Numerical experiments of the proposed chaotic system with extreme multistability

Recently, attractors in nonlinear dynamical systems have been classified into two categories: self-excited attractors and hidden attractors [12, 13]. A self-excited attractor has a basis of attraction associated with an unstable equilibrium. Common examples of chaotic systems that exhibit self-excited attractors include the Lorenz, Chen, and Rössler systems [22, 23]. In contrast, an attractor is considered hidden if its basis of attraction does not intersect with small neighborhoods of the unstable equilibrium [8].

Hidden attractors have garnered considerable attention due to their surprising dynamics as well as the potential applications, such as image encryption and random number generation [24]. Even now, a remaining open problem is to find chaotic systems with extreme multistability [25] and megastability [26, 27]. In particular, the interest is in generating chaotic attractors that are infinitely propagated on a 2D mesh and a 3D grid with special attention to those without equilibrium points [28, 29].

Therefore, research focused on hidden attractors within dynamical systems is essential for exploring this fascinating and underexplored topic.

In this work, we focus on the hidden attractors generated by the proposed chaotic system. For all simulations, we used the fourth-order Runge-Kutta numerical algorithm with a step time $h = 0.01$.

### 3.1 Extreme multistability when $Q \leq 0.25$: Chaotic system with infinitely many equilibrium points

Since this chapter focuses on chaotic systems with hidden attractors, it is essential to highlight the key differences from self-excited attractors. On the one hand, the advantages of using hidden attractors for chaos-based data encryption should be established. It means that self-excited attractors arise from hyperbolic equilibrium points and converge to the same attractor regardless of their initial conditions. As a result, even if the initial conditions are very distant from the equilibrium point in a self-excited dynamical system, the evolution of the trajectories always converges to the same attractor.

On the other hand, let us consider the following set of parameters: $P = 7$, $Q = -1$, and $R = 5$. From the results in **Figure 3**, it can be seen that, under different initial conditions, the chaotic system with infinitely many equilibrium points converges to different attractors located on a 2D mesh in the $x - y$ phase plane. It means that a

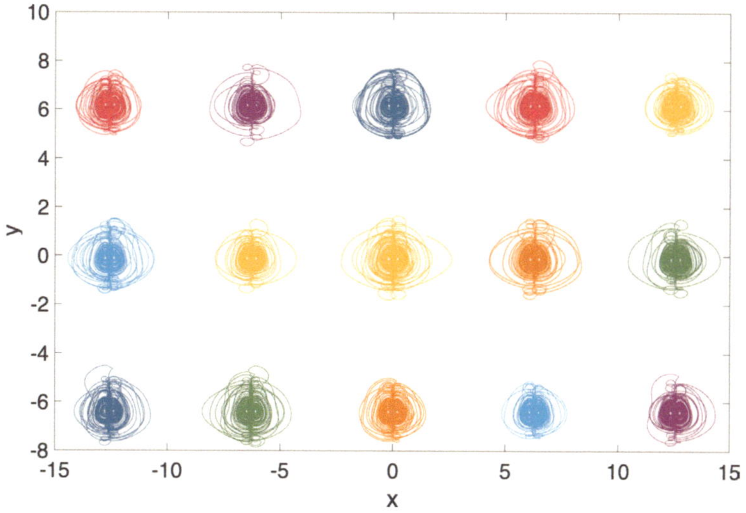


**Figure 3.**
*Infinite 2D mesh of chaotic attractors generated by the chaotic system in Eqs. (1)-(3) when it does contain infinitely many equilibrium points due to Q = -1. Each colored chaotic attractor represents a different initial condition, which varies as $(x, y, z) = (\pm n\pi, \pm n\pi, 1)$, $n = 0, \ldots$ (color figure online).*

particular chaotic attractor, e.g., the green one, appears for a determined set of initial conditions. If we change the initial conditions, the attractor would appear at another point in phase space, as shown by the navy-colored attractor. Therefore, each attractor is distributed in the $x-y$ phase plane as a function of the numerical values chosen for the initial conditions, which vary as $(x, y, z)=(\pm n\pi, \pm n\pi, 1)$, $n = 0, \ldots$. Therefore, the chaotic system satisfies Definition 3 and is considered multistable.

### 3.2 Extreme multistability when $Q > 0.25$: Chaotic system without equilibrium points

Considering $P = 7$, $Q = 0.65$, and $R = 5$, the resulting attractor for the chaotic system Eqs. (1)-(3) is given in **Figure 4**. It is noteworthy that while the same set of system parameters is used, and only by changing the initial conditions for variables $x$ and $y$, the chaotic system converges to a different chaotic attractor. It means that a particular chaotic attractor, for example, the green one, appears for a determined set of initial conditions. If we change the initial conditions, the attractor would appear at another location in phase space, as shown by the navy-colored attractor. Thus, the position of each attractor in the $x-y$ phase plane is governed by the chosen initial conditions. Since sinusoidal functions control the proposed chaotic system, the chaotic attractors appear every $2\pi$. Additionally, **Figure 5** presents the propagation of the chaotic attractors on the $x-z$ phase plane for initial conditions $-4\pi, -2\pi, 0, 2\pi, 4\pi$ in the variable $x$. It can be observed that the chaotic attractors only propagate in the $x$-axis due to the periodic signal sin. Since the variable $z$ does not depend on any periodic signal, the attractors always appear in the same position on the $z$-axis. Finally, **Figure 6** demonstrates the generation of the chaotic attractors on the $y-z$ phase plane for initial conditions $-2\pi, 0, 2\pi$ in the variable $y$.

Therefore, this chaotic system displays extreme sensitivity to initial conditions, making it highly suitable for cryptography applications. Consequently, this chaotic system belongs to the family of systems with hidden attractors, having no equilibrium

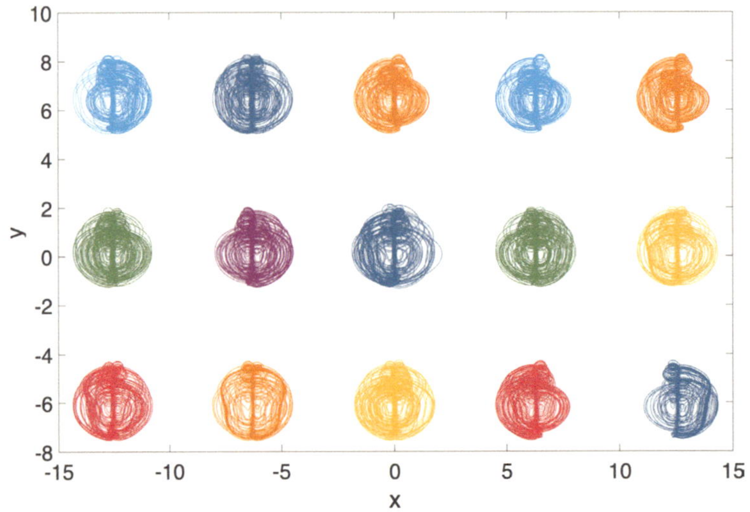


**Figure 4.**
*Infinite 2D mesh of chaotic attractors without equilibrium points produced by the proposed chaotic system when the system parameter Q = 0.65. Analogous to the previous case, the localization of the chaotic attractors on the x–y phase plane is a function of the chosen initial conditions (Color figure online).*

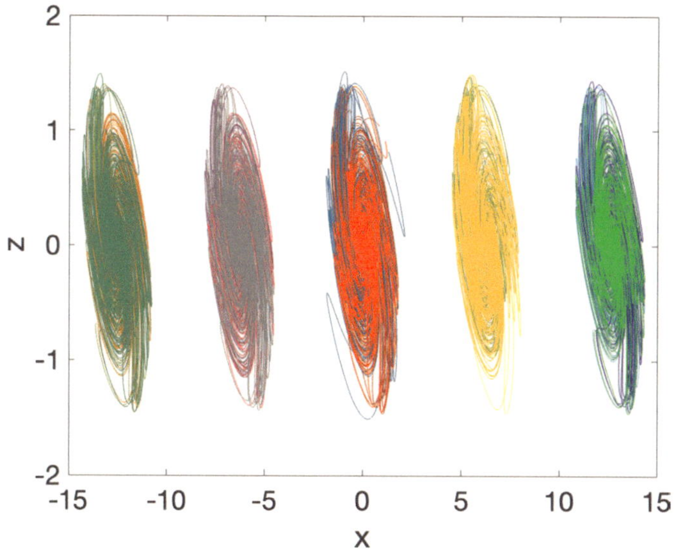


**Figure 5.**
*Infinite chaotic attractors without equilibrium points of the chaotic system in Eqs. (1)-(3) propagated in the $x-z$ phase plane when $Q = 0.65$.*

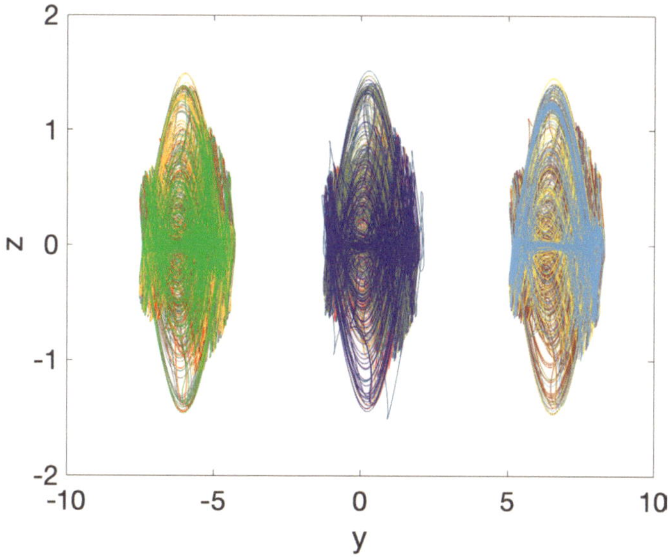


**Figure 6.**
*Chaotic attractors without equilibrium points generated by the proposed chaotic system for $Q = 0.65$. The attractors are located in the same position on the z-axis since the variable z does not depend on any periodic signal.*

points, that is, it satisfies Definition 1. Furthermore, the chaotic system exhibits extreme multistability and can consequently generate an infinite number of chaotic attractors.

Besides, we compute the Poincaré map (**Figure 7**), a crucial tool for studying and characterizing the dynamics of chaotic systems. The Poincaré map can show a single point (stable behavior), two points (periodic), and no finite $n$-points, indicating a dense set of periodic orbits —a hallmark of chaotic behavior. To understand how a

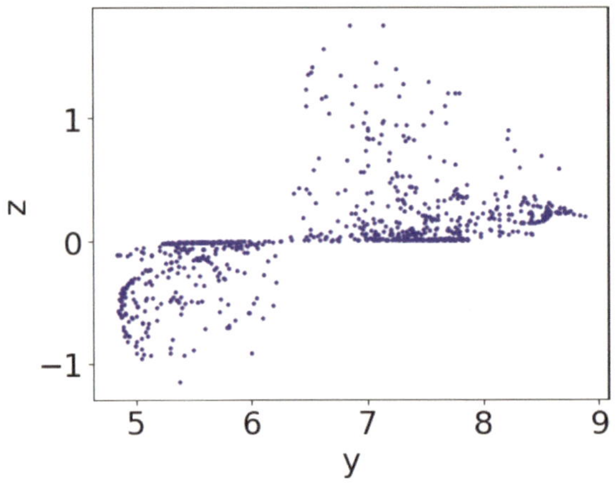


**Figure 7.**
*Poincaré map for the infinite chaotic attractors without equilibrium points generated by the proposed chaotic system with Q = 0.65. Each point on the map indicates that the trajectory crosses the hyperplane.*

Poincaré map works, the first step is to establish a $D-1$ dimensional hyperplane in the phase space of the dynamical system (without loss of generality, any of the system variables can be selected as a hyperplane). It is crucial to choose the hyperplane carefully so that, as the chaotic system trajectory evolves in state space, it crosses the plane transversely.

To obtain a suitable Poincaré surface, the trajectory of a dynamical system must successively cross the hyperplane as time evolves. Therefore, any point on the Poincaré surface is assigned to the map. Thus, the resulting Poincaré map of the proposed chaotic system, which generates an infinite 2D mesh of chaotic attractors without equilibrium points, is given in **Figure** 7. Periodic behaviors are characterized by only a pair of points on the map, while chaotic systems present a dense set of crossing points.

Chaotic systems share properties with cryptographic schemes, such as sensitivity to initial conditions, ergodicity, topological mixing, a dense set of periodic orbits, and transitivity, which make them attractive for data encryption and secure communications.

In particular, the proposed chaotic system, which has an infinite number of chaotic attractors, may have the following applications in cybersecurity:

- Block ciphers depend on linear and nonlinear operations, typically permutation and substitution, respectively. Therefore, we can utilize the property that the chaotic attractors of the proposed system can be arbitrarily generated in any region of the $x-y$ phase plane as an additional nonlinearity source to enhance the encryption of image and multimedia information.

- Since the proposed chaotic system generates infinitely many chaotic attractors, it could be used for a random number generator (RNG) where, for each attractor in the phase space, a distinct RNG can be obtained using the chaotic sequences.

- Despite the very complex behavior of the proposed chaotic system, the simplicity of the mathematical model may enable light algorithms for constrained hardware such as IoT and smart cities.

One of the main issues for the potential applications mentioned is the physical implementation of this kind of chaotic system using electronic devices. Since the physical devices, such as operational amplifiers and Field Programmable Gate Arrays (FPGAs), may induce dynamical degradation, the chaotic behaviors could be corrupted. In addition, specific hardware configurations to establish the initial conditions are also needed. However, this is not an easy task due to the multistability observed in the proposed chaotic systems. This represents an open problem. Also, chaotic systems with multistability can even enhance their properties by either adding a memristor or expanding to a fractional-order domain. On the one hand, because the memristor's internal state is defined by an additional state variable, a high-dimensional chaotic system could result. On the other hand, fractional-order derivatives cause an extra degree of freedom. Both methods may improve the encryption key space of the proposed chaotic system.

## 4. Conclusions

An elegant chaotic system with extreme multistability has been introduced in this chapter. Based on a single parameter, the chaotic system generates infinitely many chaotic attractors on a 2D mesh without equilibrium points and a surface of equilibrium points on a $x-y$ phase plane. In particular, a periodic sinusoidal function was used herein to enable the multistability. It means that, as the periodic signal propagates, the number of attractors tends to infinity. Various theoretical formulations and numerical analyses confirm the primary outcomes. For instance, the phase planes and Poincaré maps illustrate how attractors can be generated at any location of the $x-y$ phase plane. One of the central findings was to demonstrate that complex chaos can be generated from a relatively simple set of first-order differential equations, providing a simple method for studying extreme multistability. Additionally, a brief discussion on the practical applications of the proposed chaotic system in data encryption and secure communications is provided in the final section. As examined, it can be applied in block ciphers to increase nonlinearity and in random number generation to design lightweight encryption algorithms.

## Acknowledgements

The first author thanks SECIHTI for the support through the Ph.D. scholarship CVU 105600. The second and third authors acknowledge BUAP for its support via the VIEP 2025 project.

## Conflict of interest

The authors declare that they have no conflict of interest.

## Author details

Lizbeth Vargas-Cabrera[1†], Olga G. Félix-Beltrán[1*†], Jesus Manuel Munoz-Pacheco[1*†] and Viet-Thanh Pham[2†]

1 Faculty of Electronics Sciences, Benemérita Universidad Autónoma de Puebla, Puebla, Mexico

2 Faculty of Electronics Technology, Industrial University of Ho Chi Minh City, Ho Chi Minh City, Vietnam

*Address all correspondence to: olga.felix@correo.buap.mx; jesusm.pacheco@correo.buap.mx

† These authors contributed equally.

## References

[1] Lorenz EN. Deterministic nonperiodic flow. Journal of Atmospheric Sciences. 1963;**20**(2): 130-141

[2] Li C, Rajagopal K, Nazarimehr F, Liu Y. A non-autonomous chaotic system with no equilibrium. Integration. 2021; **79**:143-156

[3] Piper JR, Sprott JC. Simple autonomous chaotic circuits. IEEE Transactions on Circuits and Systems II: Express Briefs. 2010;**57**(9): 730-734

[4] Ye Y, He J. Constructing a new multi-scroll chaotic system and its circuit design. Mathematics. 2024;**12**(13):1931

[5] Wang M-m, Song X-g, Liu S-h, Zhao X-q, Zhou N-r. A novel 2D log-logistic–sine chaotic map for image encryption. Nonlinear Dynamics. 2025;**113**(3): 2867-2896

[6] Clemente-López D, Munoz-Pacheco JM, de Jesus Rangel-Magdaleno J. A review of the digital implementation of continuous-time fractional-order chaotic systems using FPGAs and embedded hardware. Archives of Computational Methods in Engineering. 2023;**30**(2): 951-983

[7] Sanchez-Lopez C, Ochoa-Montiel R, Reyes-Pérez E, Muniz-Montero C. Comparison of integer-order chaotic attractors as randomness source in collision-free robotic exploration methods. Integration. 2025;**102**:102372

[8] Munoz-Pacheco JM, Zambrano-Serrano E, Volos C, Jafari S, Kengne J, Rajagopal K. A new fractional-order chaotic system with different families of hidden and self-excited attractors. Entropy. 2018;**20**(8):564

[9] Wolf A, Swift JB, Swinney HL, Vastano JA. Determining Lyapunov exponents from a time series. Physica D: Nonlinear Phenomena. 1985;**16**(3): 285-317

[10] Zhou L, Chen F. Sil'nikov chaos of the Liu system. Chaos: An interdisciplinary. Journal of Nonlinear Science. 2008;**18**(1):013113-1-013113-5

[11] Leonov GA, Kuznetsov NV, Vagaitsev VI. Localization of hidden Chua's attractors. Physics Letters A. 2011;**375**(23):2230-2233

[12] Leonov GA, Kuznetsov NV. Hidden attractors in dynamical systems. From hidden oscillations in Hilbert–Kolmogorov, Aizerman, and Kalman problems to hidden chaotic attractor in Chua circuits. International Journal of Bifurcation and Chaos. 2013;**23**(01): 1330002

[13] Leonov GA, Kuznetsov NV, Kiseleva MA, Solovyeva EP, Zaretskiy AM. Hidden oscillations in mathematical model of drilling system actuated by induction motor with a wound rotor. Nonlinear Dynamics. 2014; **77**(1):277-288

[14] Pham V-T, Volos C, Kapitaniak T. Systems with Hidden Attractors: From Theory to Realization in Circuits. Cham, Switzerland: Springer; 2017

[15] Jafari S, Sprott JC. Simple chaotic flows with a line equilibrium. Chaos, Solitons & Fractals. 2013;**57**:79-84

[16] Zhao M, Yang Q, Zhang X. Dynamical analysis of a class of generalized chua's systems with infinitely many attractors. Computational and Applied Mathematics. 2024;**43**(6):367

[17] Dudkowski D, Jafari S, Kapitaniak T, Kuznetsov NV, Leonov GA, Prasad A. Hidden attractors in dynamical systems. Physics Reports. 2016;**637**:1-50

[18] Andrievsky BR, Kuznetsov NV, Leonov GA, Pogromsky AY. Hidden oscillations in aircraft flight control system with input saturation. IFAC Proceedings. 2013;**46**(12):75-79

[19] Wanjiang X, Shi X, Jiang H, Jianjiang Y, Zhang L, Zhuang L, et al. A simple 4D no-equilibrium chaotic system with only one quadratic term and its application in pseudo-random number generator. Chaos, Solitons & Fractals. 2024;**182**:114752

[20] Sprott JC. Strange attractors with various equilibrium types. The European Physical Journal Special Topics. 2015; **224**(8):1409-1419

[21] Subramanian R, Çiçek S, Akgul A, Adam G, Karthikeyan A, Rajagopal K. Dynamical analysis of a quadratic megastable chaotic oscillator and its application in biometric fingerprint image encryption. Complexity. 2024; **2024**(1):2005801

[22] Rössler OE. An equation for continuous chaos. Physics Letters A. 1976;**57**(5):397-398

[23] Lü J, Chen G. Generating multiscroll chaotic attractors: Theories, methods and applications. International Journal of Bifurcation and Chaos. 2006;**16**(04): 775-858

[24] Zhao G, Zhao H, Zhang Y, An X. A new memristive system with extreme multistability and hidden chaotic attractors and with application to image encryption. International Journal of Bifurcation and Chaos. 2024;**34**(01): 2450010

[25] Dinesh Vijay S, Thamilmaran K, Ishaq Ahamed A. Extreme events and multistability in nonhyperbolic chaotic system. Nonlinear Dynamics. 2024; **112**(2):1431-1438

[26] Ding D, Xinyue X, Yang Z, Zhang H, Zhu H, Liu T. Extreme multistability of fractional-order hyperchaotic system based on dual memristors and its implementation. Chaos, Solitons & Fractals. 2024;**183**:114878

[27] Li Y, Wang M, Chang H, Wang H, Chen G. A hyperchaotic memristive system with extreme multistability and conservativeness. Nonlinear Dynamics. 2024;**112**(5):3851-3868

[28] Hussan I, Zhao M, Zhang X. Two-memristor-based maps with infinitely many hyperchaotic attractors. Chaos, Solitons & Fractals. 2025;**191**:115904

[29] Zhang X, Chen M, Zhang R, Chen G. A note on the coexistence of infinitely many attractors. Chaos: An interdisciplinary. Journal of Nonlinear Science. 2025;**35**(5):051101-1-051101-5

Chapter 3

# Perspective Chapter: Beyond Computation – A Triferencial Logic for Relational Complexity

*Leonardo Lavanderos*

## Abstract

This chapter introduces the Triferencial Relational Logic (LRT) as a foundational epistemological and methodological framework for analyzing and transforming complex systems. Departing from traditional ontologies of entities and binary logic, the LRT proposes an ontology of co-implicated relations grounded in three irreducible distinctions: function, position, and sense. These dimensions allow for the mapping and interpretation of relational fields, enabling the identification of tensions, contradictions, and emergent possibilities within institutional and ecological systems. Inspired by relational epistemology, second-order cybernetics, and post-structuralist thought, the approach challenges autopoietic and computational models that reduce cognition to mechanical feedback loops. Instead, LRT integrates the observer as a constitutive part of the system, acknowledging the symbolic and situated nature of cognition. The methodology includes metarelational questions, triferencial mapping, matrices of tension, symbolic validation, and viable trajectories. Applications span across organizational governance, territorial planning, ecological restoration, and artificial intelligence, showcasing its versatility. The concept of *ecopoiesis*—understood as symbolic regeneration—is central to the framework's capacity to foster meaning and viability in fragmented or operationally empty systems. Overall, the chapter offers a transdisciplinary model that redefines the analysis of complex realities, emphasizing symbolic reconfiguration and emergent coherence as keys to sustainable transformation.

**Keywords:** triference, relational field, coimplication, function-meaning-position, emergent systemic

## 1. Introduction

In recent decades, the development of computation and formal logic has enabled significant progress in the modeling and management of complex systems. However, these approaches have shown intrinsic limitations when faced with the relational complexity inherent in living systems, organizations, and emergent processes in nature and society. Classical computational logic, based on binary operations and an epistemology focused on reducing reality to discrete, manipulable entities, is overwhelmed by phenomena where relationships cannot be reduced to unidirectional functions or linear causal chains.

In this context, the need arises for a logic capable of capturing the richness, ambiguity, and multidimensionality of the connections that shape the reality. This chapter proposes Triferencial logic as a theoretical and methodological framework aimed at addressing relational complexity from a nonreductive perspective, overcoming the limits of traditional computation, and opening up possibilities for understanding and transforming living, organizational, and technological systems.

The objective of this chapter is twofold: first, to provide a theoretical foundation for Triferencial logic, explaining its principles and differences with respect to binary logic and classical causal models; second, to demonstrate its applicability to the analysis of complex systems, proposing concrete examples in biology, ecology, organization, and artificial intelligence. The aim is to contribute to the construction of a relational paradigm that allows not only describing but also creatively intervening in fields where emergence, coevolution, and multidimensionality challenge the traditional analytical frameworks.

The development of this approach requires rethinking the very notion of difference, moving beyond the logic of binary opposition to situate oneself in a semiotic space where Triference—understood as the simultaneous dynamics of position, function, and meaning—constitutes the basis of all relational configuration. This epistemological shift also implies a reconsideration of the role of the observer, who ceases to be an external subject to become an active part of the network of relationships that he or she analyzes and transforms.

From this framework, the chapter is structured into six sections. First, the theoretical foundations and critique of classical computational models are presented. Second, Triferencial logic is developed as a formal and methodological proposal. Subsequently, concrete applications in different fields of complexity are explored. The epistemological and methodological implications of the approach are then addressed. Finally, the potential, limitations, and projections of this paradigm are discussed, concluding with a summary of the contributions and remaining challenges.

## 2. Theoretical foundations

### 2.1 Limits of classical computational logic

Classical computational logic constitutes the backbone of modern science, especially since the mathematical formalization proposed by Boole, Frege, and later Turing [1]. Its foundation lies in the binary operation, the principle of identity and non-contradiction, which allows any complex statement to be reduced to a sequence of elementary operations, facilitating its algorithmic and computational implementation. The advance of computer science and artificial intelligence has consolidated this paradigm, enabling the massive processing of information and the automation of processes in fields as diverse as biology, economics, medicine, and administration [2].

However, this approach has profound limitations when dealing with phenomena whose complexity cannot be reduced to binary operations or simple cause-effect logic. Binary logic and traditional computation have proven insufficient to explain the emergence of properties in living systems, self-organization, coevolution, or the genesis of meaning in social and cultural contexts [3]. The tendency toward discretization and fragmentation of reality prevents us from understanding the relational dynamics that shape the development of complex systems.

Several authors have pointed out the impossibility of fully modeling complexity through simple linear or recursive operations [4]. The epistemology of complexity denounces the reductionism of the computational paradigm, pointing out the need for frameworks capable of capturing the multidimensionality and constitutive interdependence of living and social systems [5].

### 2.2 Emergence of relational complexity

Since the second half of the twentieth century, the emergence of new sciences—cybernetics, systems theory, relational biology, autopoiesis theory, actor-network theory—inaugurates a fundamental epistemological shift: the transition from an ontology of entities to an ontology of relations [6]. Wiener, von Bertalanffy, Maturana, and Varela establish the bases for understanding the organization of living and artificial systems as relational processes, and not as simple aggregates of components [7].

In this context, *relational complexity* is defined not only by the quantity of elements or the density of interactions, but, fundamentally, by the quality and configuration of the links that emerge and transform over time [8]. The emphasis shifts from the static structure to the dynamic patterns of relationship and differentiation. This is where binary logic and classical computational schemes show their inadequacy, as they do not grasp the modes of codetermination, emergence, and meaning that arise in the relational framework [9].

Authors such as Morin [10], Luhmann [11], and Latour [12] have delved into the idea that reality cannot be understood from substantialist logic or from a fixed topology of objects, but rather requires a perspective capable of thematizing the process, the emergence and the co-implication of actors, elements, and symbols in the genesis of meaning. This relational perspective requires, however, a logical formalization that goes beyond the limits of the traditional binary difference [13].

### 2.3 Toward a triferencial logic

The challenge of formalizing relational complexity has led to multiple attempts to overcome binary logic. Among these, trivalent logic, fuzzy logic, and quantum computing have proposed alternatives for addressing systems with greater indeterminacy or with intermediate states [14]. However, these proposals, although valuable, usually remain within the scope of extending classical logic, without altering its ontological foundations or its basic structure of differentiation.

*Triferencial* logic emerges as a radical response to this challenge. Rather than expanding the range of values within a binary logic, Triferencial logic postulates the need to recognize *Triference as a minimal relational structure, composed of three irreducible poles: position, function, and meaning* [15]. This triad does not simply represent alternatives, but a dynamic structure of simultaneous differentiation that grounds the possibility of emergence, codetermination, and meaning in any complex system.

This approach draws on the recent developments in relational cybernetics [16] as well as on philosophical propositions in Peircean semiotics, actor-network theory, and constructivist epistemology [17]. Triference constitutes the minimal unit of meaningful differentiation, shifting the logic of one and two—typical of substantialist ontology and classical logic—toward a logic of relation and emergence.

Triferencial logic not only introduces a new way of formalizing complexity, but also implies an epistemological and methodological revolution, demanding a radical reconsideration of the bases on which knowledge and intervention in complex systems are built [18]. From this foundation, the next section will develop the formal and operational principles of Triferencial logic, as well as its difference with respect to previous models.

## 3. Triferencial logic: Foundations and principles

### 3.1 Fundamentals of trifference

Triferencial logic is based on the recognition of *Triference* as the minimal unit of significant distinction in the relational field [15]. Unlike binary logic, which is articulated on the opposition and mutual exclusion between two values (true/false, 0/1), Triferencial logic introduces a relational structure composed of three irreducible poles: *position*, *function*, and *meaning* [16]. These poles do not correspond to static categories, but represent dynamic dimensions that, in their interaction, configure every emerging form of organization, cognition, or vital process.

*Position* refers to the place that an entity, element, or relationship occupies within a given configuration. It is not an absolute point, but rather a relative reference within the relational field.

*Function* designates the role that each component plays in the dynamics of the system. The function is never intrinsic to the element but rather emerges from its connection with the other poles.

*Meaning* refers to the symbolic significance or value that a relationship or distinction acquires within the semiotic framework of the system. Meaning is not a private property, but rather an emergent quality of interaction and co-determination [17].

These three poles, in their tension and complementarity, constitute the minimal structure of differentiation capable of generating emergence, codetermination, and viability in complex systems [15]. Triference is not limited to being a mere summation of three perspectives; rather, it implies an irreducible intertwining that makes possible the multiplicity of trajectories and the emergence of the new.

### 3.2 Differences with binary logic and classical models

In classical logic, differentiation occurs by way of negation or exclusion (A/not-A). In tlogic, differentiation is constituted simultaneously by the presence and relation of three poles, none of which can be reduced to the others or eliminated without the relational structure itself disappearing [18]. Thus, the emphasis is not on separation or addition, but on coimplication.

At a formal level, while binary logic is modeled by truth tables and classical operators (AND, OR NOT), Triferencial logic requires distinction operators that operate in a three-dimensional relational topology, allowing the emergence of configurations that cannot be represented in binary space [16].

There are antecedents in trivalent logic (e.g., Łukasiewicz or Priest), but these extensions are usually interpreted as the introduction of a third value ("indeterminate," "paradox," "gray") into a still essentially binary structure [19]. On the contrary, Triferencial logic poses a completely new topological structure, where each pole has value to the extent that it is articulated and differentiated with respect to the other two, thus generating an irreducible relational matrix.

### 3.3 Relational ontology and emergence

Triferencial logic implies a paradigm shift with respect to classical ontology. It does not assume the existence of objects or entities prior to the relation; rather, the relation itself is the constitutive foundation of all existence [20]. Each pole of Triference is not a given "something," but a relational distinction that emerges in a dynamic field.

Emergence, understood as the appearance of properties or configurations that cannot be deduced from the isolated components, becomes the central phenomenon to be explained [21]. Triferencial logic offers formalism for understanding how the interaction of position, function, and meaning can give rise to new forms, trajectories, and meanings in living, organizational, social, and technological systems.

This approach has profound epistemological consequences: The observer ceases to be an external or neutral instance, to become a constitutive part of the relational field that he analyzes [22]. Thus, all knowledge is, ultimately, relational, and Triferencial logic becomes a tool not only to describe, but to intervene and reconfigure complex systems.

### 3.4 Formal and symbolic representation

Triferencial logic requires a symbolic language capable of capturing the coimplication of the three poles in each act of distinction. In algebraic terms, one can think of operators acting on ordered triplets, where the value of each component depends on the configuration of the other two [16, 18]. Similarly, graphical representation using triangles, ternary diagrams, or tension diagrams allows one to visualize the network of relationships and trajectories.

Triferencial logic results in the construction of relational matrices and maps where each node, link, or trajectory is analyzed simultaneously according to its position, function, and meaning. This perspective has proven particularly fruitful in fields such as biology, ecology, organization, and artificial intelligence, where emerging phenomena challenge linearity and classical causality [23].

## 4. Formalization of triferencial logic

To formally understand tridifferentiation, let us consider a system in which distinctions are not between objects, but emerge through a *relational function of differentiation*, held by an observer as a centralizing unit of meaning.

### 4.1 Definition of the relational distinction function

Let X be a set of states of a system, and let U be a reference unit—not a subject, but a *culturally configured condition of distinction*—then the differentiation function is defined as:

$$fU : X \times X \rightarrow [0,1] \tag{1}$$

where fU (xi, xj) represents the *relational degree with which unit U* distinguishes between states xi and xj. This function is not an objective measure, but a *situated operation* that depends on the cultural and symbolic framework of the observer.

A formalization is:

$$fU(xi, xj) = e^{-\alpha|xi - xj|} \tag{2}$$

where $\alpha$ is a *cultural parameter* that modulates the system's sensitivity to perceived difference. Higher values of $\alpha$ indicate greater sensitivity to subtle distinctions; lower values indicate greater lack of differentiation.

*Epistemic note:* This expression does not represent an objective metric of the system, but rather a *culturally mediated relational configuration*.

## 5. Tridifferentiation and relational organization

In LRT, the minimal unit of configuration is not an ordered pair (xi, xj), as in binary logic, but a *relational triad* (xi, xj, xk). It is this triad that sustains the differentiation process as an event.

Given a set $X = \{x1, x2, x3\}$, the *unit of Trifrential differentiation* can be defined as:

$$DU = fU(x1, x2) + fU(x2, x3) + fU(x3, x1) \tag{3}$$

This structure ensures that:

Each difference is *co-sustained by two others*.

There are no isolated units: every identity is *the effect of a network of relationally activated distinctions*.

Tridifferentiation does not define elements, but rather culturally *sustained dynamic configurations of difference*.

### 5.1 Application to complex systems and neural networks

In organizational, cognitive, or biological networks, LRT allows for modeling structures without relying on interaction metrics between discrete nodes (as in classical cybernetics). Here, the relevant issue is not the intrinsic value of each node, but rather *how its meaning emerges from the network of relational distinctions*.

Key principles in this approach:

A node has no identity in itself: *its meaning is relational and emerges by tridifferentiation*.

Organizational alignment does not occur through the adjustment of parts, but through *coherence in the structure of collectively held distinctions*.

The cohesion and viability of the system depend on the stability of the Triferencial relationships, not on the individual elements.

This approach allows *the organization to be modeled without falling into the subject-object dichotomy*, while ensuring that *any distinction is relational, situated, and culturally sustained.*

Triferencial Relational Logic (LRT) offers a conceptual and methodological framework that addresses the intrinsic relational complexity of both natural and artificial systems. In complex systems science, LRT enables the mapping of relational fields beyond mere quantitative connectivity patterns, integrating:

- *Position*: the structural location of nodes, actors, or components within a network or ecosystem.

- *Function*: the role each element plays in sustaining systemic dynamics.

- *Meaning*: the emergent symbolic significance of relationships within cultural, ecological, or organizational contexts.

For example, in ecological systems, LRT has been applied to the *restoration of high Andean wetlands*, mapping not only species distributions (position) and ecological roles (function) but also their cultural and symbolic meanings for local communities (meaning), thus informing regenerative interventions that integrate conservation biology and ethnoecology [24, 25].

In organizational systems, LRT has been utilized to model *succession processes in family businesses*, where viability depends not only on roles and structures but also on the symbolic legitimacy of leadership transitions [26].

In the field of *artificial neural networks (ANNs)*, LRT opens the possibility of designing Triferencial architectures. Traditional ANNs model input-output relationships through weighted connections and activation functions (position and function). By integrating a *meaning layer*, networks could map data representations to symbolic categories or cultural ontologies, enhancing the explainability and cognitive alignment. This is particularly relevant in domains such as ecological classification, where outputs require cultural interpretation (e.g., identifying a wetland not only as a habitat type but also as an ancestral gathering place) [27].

### 5.2 Comparison between Triferencial Relational Logic, Paracoherent Logic, and the Spencer-Brown Laws of Form

Triferencial Relational Logic (TRL) proposes a radical break with the foundations of traditional logic by shifting the focus from objects and propositions to *the relational act of distinction* as the founding operation of meaning. In this context, it is pertinent to compare it with two non-classical logical proposals: *Paracoherent Logic*, which allows for the coexistence of contradictions, and G. Spencer-Brown's *Laws of Form*, which articulate a logic of distinction through boundary marking.

### 5.3 Triferencial Relational Logic (TRL)

- *Central foundation*: The difference does not exist in the elements or in their objective relationships but rather *emerges as a relational act of a culturally conditioned observer*.
- *Minimal structure*: There are no binary distinctions. Every distinction requires three components: xi, xj, and a unit U that distinguishes them using the function fU.
- *Distinction function*:

$$fU(xi, xj) = Relational\ distinction\ as\ a\ cultural\ act \tag{4}$$

- *Cultural character*: The distinction is neither universal nor timeless; it is situated in a history of cultural configurations.
- *Temporality*: The distinction occurs in time and can be transformed according to the historical-cultural context of the observer.
- *Role of the observer*: It is an *active condition* of distinction. Without it, differentiation is not possible.

### 5.4 Paracoherent logic

- *Central Foundation*: It introduces the possibility of maintaining logical contradictions without the system collapsing. The goal is not to resolve the contradiction, but rather *to incorporate it as a constituent part of contextual coherence*.

- *Minimal structure*: Binary (true/false) but allows the coexistence of affirmation and negation under certain conditions.

- *Contradiction tolerance*: A formula can be simultaneously true and false without invalidating the system.

- *Contextuality*: Coherence is not defined by the exclusion of contradiction, but by its *integration into a coherent whole from the point of view of the system*.

- *Temporality*: Flexible; conditions of validity may vary, but do not depend directly on the observer's cultural history.

- *Observer role*: Present, but implicit. Their role is more passive; they recognize contradictions without having to resolve them.

### 5.5 Laws of Form (Spencer-Brown)

- *Central foundation*: Every form emerges through a *distinction*: drawing a boundary between the "inside" and the "outside" of an operation.

- *Minimal structure*: Binary. The distinction operator generates two domains (marked/unmarked).

- *Form of distinction*: distinction $\Rightarrow$ difference between marked and unmarked

- *Self-reference*: The system allows for *reentry*, that is, the possibility of a distinction being applied to itself.

- *Universality*: Distinctions are considered *universal and timeless*: they do not depend on the cultural context or the observer.

- *Role of the observer*: Implicit in the act of drawing the distinction, but *not thematized as a culturally situated instance*.

### 5.6 Ternary, quaternary, and multivalued logics

The challenge of formalizing complex systems has led to the development of alternative logical frameworks beyond classical bivalent logic. Among these, ternary, quaternary, and multivalued logics have gained prominence in the recent decades due to their capacity to model systems with intermediate or multiple states, thus overcoming the limitations of binary opposition.

Ternary logic, also known as trivalent logic, introduces a third value in addition to true and false, commonly interpreted as "indeterminate" or "unknown."

This framework was initially formalized by Łukasiewicz in the early twentieth century and has since been explored in quantum computation, decision theory, and logic programming for dealing with incomplete information [1]. Recent applications include modeling indeterminate quantum states and optimizing neural network architectures to reduce computational complexity and energy consumption [2].

Quaternary logic extends the principle by introducing four discrete logical states, enabling higher information density in electronic circuits and memory storage. In contemporary computing, quaternary logic has been proposed to improve the design of multiple-valued logic (MVL) circuits, which reduce the number of interconnections and enhance operational speed compared to binary-based systems [3]. Research has shown that quaternary logic can achieve significant reductions in transistor count and power dissipation in integrated circuit design, crucial for advanced AI hardware implementation [4].

Multivalued logic (MVL) generalizes these approaches by allowing any finite or infinite number of logical values. Fuzzy logic is one of its best-known forms, introduced by Zadeh, where truth values are represented as continuous degrees between 0 and 1, enabling the modeling of vagueness, gradation, and uncertainty in real-world phenomena [5]. Current MVL research addresses quantum computing gates with multiple levels [6] and the design of cognitive architectures capable of learning from graded inputs, supporting advances in explainable AI and cognitive robotics [7].

However, while ternary, quaternary, and multivalued logics expand the range of representable states within formal systems, they do not fundamentally challenge the ontological assumptions of classical logic based on substantial entities and pre-existing differences. Instead, they extend state spaces within the same underlying structure. In contrast, Triferencial Logic proposes a radical shift by situating difference itself as an emergent relational act sustained by an observer, redefining both the epistemological and ontological foundations of logic and its application to complex, emergent, and symbolically mediated systems, as summarized in **Table 1**.

### 5.7 Key differences

1. *LRT vs. Paracoherent Logic:*

    - LRT does not seek to resolve or tolerate contradictions, but to show that difference itself does not preexist, but rather emerges relationally from a cultural observer.

    - Paracoherent logic maintains the binary structure, but relaxes the exclusion rules, while LRT transcends binary logic, incorporating the third differentiating instance.

2. *LRT vs. Laws of Form:*

    - While Spencer-Brown conceives of distinction as a universal structural act, LRT holds that every distinction is culturally sustained, and that there is no difference without context and history.

    - In the Laws of Form, the distinction once drawn has absolute validity; in LRT, the distinction is transient, contextual, and observer-dependent.

| Aspect | Triferencial logic (LRT) | Paracoherent logic | Laws of form (Spencer-Brown) | Ternary logic | Quaternary logic | Multivalued logic (MVL) |
|---|---|---|---|---|---|---|
| *Origin of the difference* | Relational act sustained by the cultural observer | Contextual coexistence of affirmation and negation | Marking a boundary between the internal and the external | Introduction of a third value ("indeterminate") | Introduction of a fourth logical state | Multiplicity of logical values, including continuous degrees |
| *Minimum unit* | Triad: xi, xj, U | Binary pair (A / ¬A) | Distinction operation (form/non-form) | Three discrete states | Four discrete states | N states (finite or infinite) |
| *Role of the observer* | Active, cultural, and temporal condition | Passive and contextual, allows contradiction | Implicit; not themed as an agent | Implicit; not thematized | Implicit; not thematized | Implicit or parameterized depending on application |
| *Ontology* | Rejects all ontology; relation has no existence in itself | Maintains coherence without defined ontology | Implies a structural, universal, and formal logic | Substantialist extended with third state | Substantialist extended with fourth state | Substantialist or gradational depending on MVL |
| *Temporality* | Situated, dynamic, culturally mediated distinction | Flexible, but not historical or cultural | Timeless; distinction is valid once made | Timeless | Timeless | Variable; discrete or continuous depending on application |
| *Culturality* | High: distinction depends on symbolic and historical frameworks | Moderate: coherence is contextual but not necessarily cultural | Null: operations are formal and context-independent | Null | Null | Variable; fuzzy MVL incorporates cultural degrees in interpretation |
| *Handling contradiction* | Does not thematize contradiction; focuses on emerging difference | Central: allows contradictions without logical collapse | Recognizes paradoxes in reentry but does not address them ethically | Introduces indeterminacy as a third state | Does not consider contradiction as a central property | Fuzzy MVL models gradation and ambiguity, not formal contradiction |
| *Epistemology* | Relational, situated, constructive | Contextual and open | Formalist, structural | Formalist extended | Formalist extended | Formalist, gradational, or constructive (fuzzy) |

**Table 1.**
*Comparative analysis of logical frameworks.*

3. *On relational existence:*

- LRT explicitly maintains that relation has no ontology. It is not an entity, nor a link between entities. It is an act of differentiating configuration, culturally sustained.
- The other two logics, on the other hand, admit more stable or abstract forms of structuring, although not necessarily reified.

## 6. Notation and operations of Triferencial Relational Logic (TRL)

LRT is built on the fundamental principle that difference is not a property of elements, nor a relationship between them, but rather a situated relational act conducted by a culturally determined unit of distinction (U), treated here as the operator that performs relational differentiation. The formalization of this logic requires a specific notation that allows for the expression of Triferential operations, cultural functions, and dynamic relational structures, as detailed in **Table 2**.

### 6.1 Fundamental operations

Tridifferentiation Operator ▷.
The basic operation of the LRT is expressed as:

$$R(xi, xj, U) = xi \triangleright xj|U \tag{5}$$

This operation indicates that the difference between *xi y xj does not exist by itself*, but is *activated by the relational act of the* observer U.

The *tridifferentiation operator* expresses the act by which a *non-pre-existing difference* is generated by the relational intervention of an observer U. This operator articulates three components: two distinctions xi and xj, and the unit of differentiation U.

$$(xi, xj, U) \triangleright DU(xi, xj) \tag{6}$$

| Symbol | Meaning |
|---|---|
| xi, xj | Active distinctions (not fixed entities, but effects of differentiation) |
| OR | Observer unit (condition of possibility of the relational act) |
| fU | Cultural function of distinction, historically situated |
| DU(xi, xj) | Degree of distinction generated by U between xi and xj |
| ▷ | Tridifferentiation operator (relational act between two distinctions and a U) |
| ∇ U | Relational difference operator (differentiation gradient) |
| ∘ | Relational composition (chaining acts of distinction) |
| ↔ | Relational inversion (change of observer's perspective) |
| ⊕ | Relational overlap (combination of multiple distinctions) |
| ∅ | Absence of the observer |

**Table 2.**
*Notation of Triferencial Relational Logic (TRL).*

or explicitly:

$$xi \triangleright xj|U \Rightarrow DU(xi, xj) = \alpha U \cdot (|xi - U| + |xj - U|)$$

Where:

- $\triangleright$: denotes the *relational act* by which the observer U generates a distinction between xi and xj.
- | xi−U | and | xj − U |: represent the *relational distance* between each element and the observer's frame of reference.
- DU(xi, xj): is the *value of the relational distinction* held by U.
- αU: is the cultural sensitivity of the observer, as in the operator ∇ U.

*Conceptual interpretation:*
The difference is not "between" xi and xj, but in *how the observer positions himself relationally with respect to both*. The distinction does not exist without the Triferencial act. There is no distinction without a third party to sustain it.

### 6.2 Operator properties

*Essential relationality*:

$$xi \triangleright xj|\varnothing = 0 \tag{7}$$

Without an observer, there is no possible distinction.
*Cultural dependence:*

$$D < U1(xi, xj) \neq DU2(xi, xj) \tag{8}$$

Two different observers can produce different distinctions about the same elements.
*Configurative asymmetry*:

$$xi \triangleright xj|U \neq xj \triangleright xi|U \tag{9}$$

The order of distinctions matters if fU is asymmetrical, which is common in cultural structures.

$$\nabla \mathrm{U}(\mathrm{xi}, \mathrm{xj}) = \alpha \mathrm{U} \cdot |\mathrm{xi} - \mathrm{xj}| \tag{10}$$

## 7. Compound relational operations

### 7.1 Relational composition ∘

tridifferentiation acts when they share an intermediate distinction

$$(xi \triangleright xj|U) \circ (xj \triangleright xk|U) = xi \triangleright xk|U \tag{11}$$

This means that observer U can *make distinctions in sequence*, connecting multiple elements through successive relational acts. Relational composition is *transitive*, provided the same observer is maintained and the conditions of cultural coherence of the system are respected.

### 7.2 Relational investment ↔

The relationship of tridifferentiation can be reversed if the observer changes his interpretive position:

$$xi \triangleright xj|U \leftrightarrow xj \triangleright xi|U \tag{12}$$

However, *this inversion can modify the value of the distinction* if the cultural function fU is not symmetrical:

$$fU(xi,xj) \neq fU(xj,xi) \tag{13}$$

This reflects that *the difference is not intrinsic to the pair* but depends on how the observer orients his relational act.

### 7.3 Relational overlay

When two acts of tridifferentiation occur simultaneously (or are sustained concurrently), their effects may combine:

$$DU(xi,xj) \oplus DU(xk,xl) = \alpha U \cdot (|xi - xj| + |xk - xl|) \tag{14}$$

This operator allows modeling situations where multiple distinctions affect the observer's perception or action, such as in complex semiotic, social, or organizational phenomena.

### 7.4 General properties of relational operations

See **Table 3**.

| Property | Symbol | Description |
|---|---|---|
| Observer dependence | OR | Without an observer, there is no relational act or distinction. |
| No symmetry | $\nabla U(xi, xj) \neq \nabla U(xj,xi)$ | The orientation of the differentiating act influences the perceived value. |
| Compositionality | ∘ | Tridifferentiations can be chained sequentially. |
| Overlap | ⊕ | Multiple acts of distinction can be combined to form configurations. |
| Culturality | fU | The sensitivity and form of the differentiating act depend on the cultural framework. |

**Table 3.**
*General properties of relational operations.*

### 7.5 Extended notation for systems with multiple observers

In complex systems involving multiple observers—such as epistemic communities, organizational networks, or social collectives—each observer Uk operates with a cultural function fUk of their own, which cannot be directly added to the others without losing the relational structure that links them. In this context, the degree of distinction is not obtained by aggregation, but by the relational composition of differentiating perspectives.

$$D_{config}(xi, xj) = F\left(\left\{f_{U_k}(xi, xj)\right\}_{k=1}^{n}\right) \tag{15}$$

Where:

- $F$ is a *relational configuration function*, not a sum, which models the emergent coherence or tension between the distinctions generated by different observers.
- This function may involve conditions of *structural coupling*, *cultural coherence*, or even *conflict of codifications*, depending on the relational domain.

### 7.6 Triferencial formalization of organizational coherence

In a complex organization composed of multiple cultural observers (e.g., teams, areas, leaderships, internal communities), organizational coherence is not defined by the sum of individual distinctions, but by the emerging consistency between the acts of relational distinction conducted by each cultural unit around a shared situation or problem.

Configuration space:

$$D_{org} = \left\{f_{U_k}(xi, xj) | k = 1, 2, \ldots, n\right\} \tag{16}$$

Each observer $U_k$ holds a relational distinction $f_{U_k}(xi, xj)$, which expresses his or her culturally situated way of differentiating between xi and xj within the system.

### 7.7 Relational consistency operator

We propose to define Triferencial organizational coherence as:

$$C_{org}(xi, xj) = 1 - \sigma\left(\left\{f_{U_k}(xi, xj)\right\}_{k=1}^{n}\right) \tag{17}$$

σ is a (nonlinear) relational dispersion operator that measures the dissonance between observers' cultural roles. It can be defined as the normalized relational variance, or as the relative semiotic deviation from a cultural center of gravity.

Corg ∈ [0,1], where 1 indicates maximum coherence (all observers generate similar distinctions) and 0 indicates total dissonance (each observer holds divergent distinctions).

Operational example with average distance:

$$\sigma = \frac{1}{n(n-1)} \sum_{k \neq l} \left| f_{U_k}(xi, xj) - f_{U_l}(xi, xj) \right| \tag{18}$$

And therefore:

$$C_{org}(xi, xj) = 1 - \sigma \tag{19}$$

This value does not represent an "average" in the classical sense, but rather an *emerging coherence* based on the *Triferencial configuration of distinctions*.

*Relational interpretation*

- If everyone $f_{U_k}$ converges on a similar distinction, a strong organizational coherence is generated, facilitating communication, coordination, and management (CO4).

- If observers hold incompatible distinctions, organizational dissonance arises, which can generate conflict, ambiguity, or institutional fragmentation.

*Summary of fundamental operations*

- The $\nabla$ *U operator* quantifies the relational degree of differentiation under a cultural framework.

- The *operator* $\triangleright$ emphasizes that the distinction does not preexist but *emerges in the relational act*.

- The *composition* $\circ$ allows for the chaining of acts of distinction.

- The $\leftrightarrow$ *inversion* allows the observer's interpretive orientation to be reorganized.

- The *superposition* $\oplus$ allows to model concurrent distinctions.

- The *extended notation* integrates multiple observers, allowing the capture of collective epistemic configurations.

## 8. Applications and examples

### 8.1 Biology: Emergence of living things and ecopoiesis

Triferencial logic allows us to approach the emergence of living from a radically relational perspective, overcoming the autopoietic paradigm which, although relevant in its time, remains anchored in binary distinctions and a closed operationalism [15]. *Ecopoiesis*, conceptualized by Lavanderos and Malpartida, offers an alternative framework where life is not understood as mere self-productivity, but as the emergence of living configurations from the tension and Triferencial co-implication of position, function, and meaning [24].

In this approach, a living unit exists only as part of a relational trinity; if two poles are occupied by non-living units, the third extracts differences and activates trajectories that cannot be understood from linear causality or from closed self-reference. Viability, regeneration, and biological memory thus emerge from the dynamic articulation between the three poles, displacing any substantialist or object-based explanation [25].

Ecopoietic analysis allows, for example, mapping the regeneration of biological communities, understanding ecological thresholds, and designing restoration interventions that do not depend on functional "essences" but on Triferencial fields of symbiotic emergence [28].

### 8.2 Ecotome analysis and triferencial restoration

The concept of *ecotome*, developed by Malpartida and Lavanderos, shifts the classical notion of ecosystem—centered on predetermined objects and functions—toward a relational, symbiotic, and Triferencial reading [25]. Here, each node of the ecotome is analyzed according to its position in the plot, the function it plays in the regeneration trajectories, and the symbolic meaning it mobilizes for the biological and human community.

Triferencial logic allows us to map ecosystem configurations and vulnerabilities not as "losses" or "faults" but as tensions between poles, identifying the viable trajectories for relational recomposition or collapse. Thus, ecological restoration ceases to be a mechanical or engineering operation and becomes a symbiotic process of relational co-creation, where the observer is an active part of the field of emergence [28].

### 8.3 Organization and governance: Legitimacy and succession from the trifference

In the field of organization and governance, Triferencial logic underpins a living, nonlinear interpretation of structure, displacing traditional hierarchical approaches and classical functionalism [16, 29]. Living organizations are configured as dynamic networks, in which viability depends on the ability to articulate—and not simply add—position, function, and meaning in each node, link, and trajectory [26].

Critical processes such as succession or organizational transformation cannot be reduced to the transfer of positions or functions; they require the regeneration of collective meaning and the symbolic recomposition of the relational field. Triferencial maps allow for the identification of nodes of legitimacy, blocked trajectories, and symbolic vulnerabilities, offering the unprecedented input for relational management and strategic intervention [16, 26].

### 8.4 Artificial intelligence and relational agent design

The development of adaptive artificial intelligence requires abandoning the classic binary model and causal rule-based programming. Triferencial logic and ecopoiesis open up the possibility of building agents capable of learning and operating not only based on data or hierarchical positions but also based on symbolic trajectories and living configurations. Thus, agents can reconfigure themselves in the face of new tensions, activate emerging meanings, and participate in the co-construction of complex solutions in fields as diverse as health, territorial management, and decentralized governance (**Figure 1**).

### 8.5 Illustrative example: Triferencial restoration in high Andean plains

In the ecological restoration, Triferencial analysis has allowed the identification of living trajectories of biological regeneration, symbiotic vulnerabilities, and ecological thresholds, which are invisible to classical functional analysis or species inventories (**Figure 2**) [28]. Each intervention is designed considering the Triferencial field of

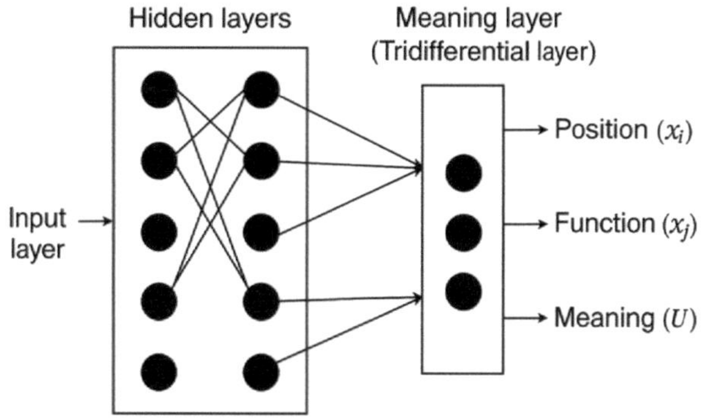


**Figure 1.**
*Triferencial Artificial Intelligence Agents. Conceptual representation of adaptive artificial intelligence agents designed under Triferencial logic and ecopoiesis frameworks, integrating data, hierarchical positions, and symbolic trajectories.*

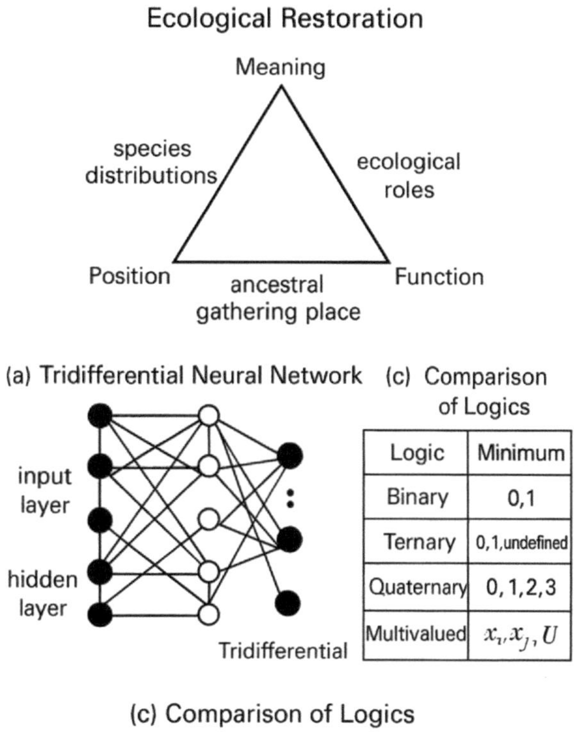


**Figure 2.**
*Triferencial Analysis in High Andean Plains Restoration. Triferencial mapping of ecological restoration interventions in high Andean plains, integrating ecosystem position, functional role in regeneration, and symbolic meaning for human and non-human communities. This approach reveals living trajectories, symbiotic vulnerabilities, and ecological thresholds invisible to classical functional analyses, enabling adaptive and legitimate sustainability solutions.*

position (ecosystem location), function (role in regeneration or ancestral memory), and meaning (symbolic value for human and non-human communities), enabling adaptive and legitimate solutions for sustainability [24, 25].

## 9. Epistemological and methodological implications

### 9.1 Epistemological rupture: From object to relationship

Triferencial logic and ecopoiesis constitute a break with classical epistemologies, in which knowledge is based on the existence of independent objects or entities [15, 16]. In the Triferencial paradigm, the starting point is the relationship: All existence is the result of a field of differences that are dynamically configured between position, function, and meaning [24]. It is not a matter of describing what "there is" as an inventory of entities, but of understanding how the frameworks and trajectories arise, are configured and reconfigured from differential interaction [18].

This approach implies abandoning the search for "essences," linear causes, or immutable substances. Research interest is not directed toward isolated entities, but toward trajectories, tensions, living differences, dynamic configurations, and the symbolic conditions of emergence and viability of these frameworks [19, 25]. Triferencial research is thus inseparable from intervention since analysis itself is a way of activating or inhibiting relational trajectories.

### 9.2 Observer involvement and coemergence of meaning

Unlike classical epistemology, which positions the observer as an external and neutral subject, Triferencial logic recognizes the *constitutive implication of the observer* in the relational field [16]. Knowledge is inseparable from the act of distinction, selection, and configuration that the observer conducts when participating in the framework of living tensions. Meaning is never given in advance nor is it external to the process, but rather *it co-emerges* with the configuration that is being analyzed and intervened in [15].

This epistemological implication displaces the figure of the knowing subject and replaces it with that of the *relational agent*, that is, the one who is simultaneously configurator and configured, an active part of the symbiotic web of emergence and transformation [17, 25]. In this way, all research is, at the same time, an inquiry into the conditions of possibility of knowing, intervening in and sustaining symbolic configurations.

### 9.3 Triferencial methodology: From diagnosis to intervention

The Triferencial method is structured around distinct steps that allow for the analysis and reorganization of complex fields, beyond mere description:

1. *Formulation of the meta-cognitive question:* The process begins with an interrogation aimed at opening up possibilities, without seeking substantial causes or fixed responsibilities [24].

2. *Relational mapping:* The nodes, trajectories, and main tensions are identified and represented, always considering the difference in position, function, and meaning [16, 28].

3. *Construction of the Triferencial matrix:* Each node and trajectory are analyzed and evaluated in relation to the three poles, allowing the visualization of configurations, blockages, and emerging potentialities [15, 29].

4. *Extraction of viable trajectories:* From the previous analysis, trajectories and solutions that emerge from the symbolic rearticulation of the relational field are identified [26].

5. *Symbolic validation and transformation:* The legitimacy and viability of the proposed solutions are evaluated, considering their capacity to regenerate meaning, avoid functional or positional closure, and activate the emergence of new living configurations [25].

This methodology has proven effective in reorganizing symbolic fields, overcoming epistemological blocks and promoting unprecedented, legitimate, and sustainable solutions in areas such as ecological restoration, territorial governance, organizational transformation, and adaptive artificial intelligence systems [28].

### 9.4 Transdisciplinarity and hermeneutic potential

The Triferencial approach, by shifting the center of gravity from the entity to the relationship, opens up the possibility of a living transdisciplinarity [25, 30]. Complex problems, which go beyond the boundaries of traditional disciplines, can be addressed from configurations of meaning that integrate biological, ecological, organizational, technological, and symbolic perspectives [18, 31].

Triferencial method has a hermeneutic potential: It is not limited to explaining or predicting but allows for the interpretation and re-signification of fields of action, reconstructing the symbolic horizon from which both problems and solutions emerge [29]. This capacity for re-signification is fundamental in contexts of crisis, transition, or emergency, where previous meanings have become insufficient or even toxic for relational viability.

## 10. Discussion

### 10.1 Triferencial logic and ecopoiesis

Triferencial logic and ecopoiesis represent a radical shift in the analysis and intervention of complex configurations. By shifting the focus of interest from fixed objects, functions, or positions to the symbolic articulation of trajectories, a new way of understanding emergence, transformation, and sustainability is enabled in fields as diverse as biology, ecology, organization, and the design of artificial intelligence [15, 24, 29].

One of the main contributions of the Triferencial approach is that it allows the identification of tensions and trajectories hidden in traditional analyses, where the fragmented or causal view leaves unaddressed symbolic or emergent dimensions crucial to the viability of a relational field [25, 28]. Thus, the ability to map, intervene, and reconfigure frameworks from the position, function, and meaning has demonstrated its effectiveness in adaptive management, symbolic regeneration, and the resolution of organizational or ecological crises [26, 27].

### 10.2 Critical distance from autopoiesis and classical cybernetics

Despite certain affinities with cybernetics and systems theory, Triferencial logic distances itself methodologically and epistemologically from autopoiesis and classical cybernetics [16, 24]. While autopoiesis focuses its explanation on operational closure and functional reproduction, Triferencial logic shifts the emphasis toward symbolic opening and the emergence of meaning [24, 25]. Furthermore, the Triferencial structure allows us to understand configurations and trajectories that remain invisible to binary and closed models.

Similarly, the concept of ecopoiesis, unlike autopoiesis, does not presuppose a closed self-production, but rather symbiotic co-production and co-implication, where viability and emergence depend on the dynamic and multiple interaction of nodes, trajectories, and horizons of meaning [24, 25]. In this sense, Triferencial logic constitutes a platform to address complexity without falling into functionalism or operational reductionism.

### 10.3 Comparison with actor-network approaches and constructivism

Triferencial logic shares with Latour's actor-network theory and radical constructivism the critique of substantialist ontologies and the openness to multiple configurations and trajectories [12, 17, 30]. However, it introduces a fundamental difference: While actor-network theory privileges the multiplicity of actors and connections without a formal structuring principle, Triferencial logic offers a specific conceptual and operational matrix (position, function, and meaning) to map and reorganize symbolic and relational fields [15, 16].

In contrast to radical constructivism, which questions the foundation of knowledge but does not always offer tools for practical intervention, the Triferencial approach provides a structured method for reorganizing complex fields and generating novel solutions [17, 29]. This methodological potential has been demonstrated in a variety of applications, from ecological restoration to organizational transformation [25, 26, 28].

## 11. Triferencial logic

Triferencial logic and ecopoiesis open up unprecedented horizons, and they also present challenges and limitations. One of these is the difficulty of formalizing symbolic trajectories in fields where distinctions can be unstable or where conditions of emergence vary rapidly. Furthermore, applying the method requires a learning and training process for both researchers and relational agents, who must abandon interpretive habits based on fixed entities and linear relationships.

Triferencial logic, by its very relational nature, challenges disciplinary languages and methodologies, forcing the construction of new frameworks for collaboration and co-learning [25, 30]. However, it is precisely in these challenges that its transformative potential lies, by offering a path for symbolic reconstruction, crisis management, and the promotion of viability in complex fields.

### 11.1 Projections and theoretical-methodological potential

Triferencial logic and ecopoiesis open up new lines of research and practice for the analysis, intervention, and design of constantly changing relational fields [24, 29]. Their applications, still expanding, allow us to imagine a radical transformation of the biological, ecological, organizational, cognitive, and technological sciences, placing emergence, meaning, and symbolic co-implication at the center of inquiry and action.

The potential of these approaches lies in their ability to articulate theory, method, and intervention in a single movement, enabling the continuous redefinition and sustainable living of ever-changing relational frameworks [15, 25, 29]. Their future development will depend on the consolidation of epistemic communities capable of sustaining, deepening, and renewing the Triferencial relational paradigm in critical and creative dialog with other emerging approaches.

## 12. Conclusion

Triferencial logic and ecopoiesis represent a profound epistemological and methodological break with traditional analytical frameworks. By focusing inquiry and intervention on the dynamic configuration of position, function, and meaning, these approaches displace any search for grounding in fixed entities, linear causes, or substantial essences [15, 24, 25]. Knowledge and action are reconfigured as processes of distinction, articulation, and symbolic emergence, where viability, regeneration, and sustainability depend on the quality of the tensions and trajectories that unfold in each relational field [16, 29].

Triferencial logic is expressed in its capacity to identify blockages, visualize unprecedented trajectories and legitimize transformation processes in fields as diverse as ecology, biology, organization, and artificial intelligence [24–26]. Overcoming functionalist reductionism and opening up to living transdisciplinarity allows for addressing complex problems beyond the limitations imposed by disciplinary approaches and traditional causal models [30].

Likewise, the recognition of the constitutive involvement of the observer and the centrality of symbolic resignification relocates the place of knowledge and intervention, displacing any pretense of neutrality or externality. The relational agent thus emerges as a co-configurator and co-emergent of the symbolic trajectories and fields that it investigates and transforms [17].

Among the future challenges is the need to develop languages, methodologies, and epistemic communities capable of sustaining and expanding the Triferencial paradigm, fostering critical collaboration and collective creativity [25, 30]. The path opened by Triferencial logic and ecopoiesis invites us to reinvent both research and action, placing symbolic emergence and relational co-implication at the very heart of living organization, strategic intervention, and the sustainability of fields in transformation [15, 24, 29].

## Author details

Leonardo Lavanderos
Sintesys Corporación, Centro de Ecología Aplicada S.A Metropolitan Technological University, Observatory of the Territory, Santiago, Chile

*Address all correspondence to: l.lavanderos@sintesys.cl

## References

[1] Turing AM. Computing machinery and intelligence. Mind. 1950;**59**(236): 433-460

[2] Boole G. An Investigation of the Laws of Thought. London: Walton and Maberly; 1854

[3] Kauffman S. The Origins of Order: Self-Organization and Selection in Evolution. New York: Oxford University Press; 1993

[4] Morin E. Introduction to Complex Thought. Barcelona: Gedisa; 2001

[5] Mitchell M. Complexity: A Guided Tour. New York: Oxford University Press; 2009

[6] Wiener N. Cybernetics: Or Control and Communication in the Animal and the Machine. Paris: Hermann & Cie; 1948

[7] von Bertalanffy L. General System Theory. New York: George Braziller; 1968

[8] Maturana H, Varela F. Autopoiesis and Cognition: The Realization of the Living. Dordrecht: D. Reidel Publishing; 1980

[9] Luhmann N. Social Systems. Stanford: Stanford University Press; 1996

[10] Morin E. La méthode. Paris: Seuil; 1977

[11] Luhmann N. Theory of Society. Stanford: Stanford University Press; 2012

[12] Latour B. Reassembling the Social: An Introduction to Actor-Network-Theory. Oxford: Oxford University Press; 2005

[13] Cybersemiotics BS. Why Information Is Not Enough! Toronto: University of Toronto Press; 2008. 498 p. (Toronto Studies in Semiotics and Communication). ISBN: 978-1442626362

[14] Zadeh LA. Fuzzy sets. Information and Control. 1965;**8**(3):338-353. DOI: 10.1016/S0019-9958(65)90241-X

[15] Lavanderos L, Oliva I. From distinction to configuration: Complexity, evaluation, and learning from a relational perspective. Estudios Pedagógicos. 2012; **38**(1):273-283. DOI: 10.4067/S0718-07052012000100016

[16] Hormazábal F, Lavanderos L, Malpartida A. Biocybernetic model for the diagnosis and treatment of chronic pain: An approximation from cognitive neurosciences and the theory of complexity. Kybernetes. 2021;**50**(2): 369-385. DOI: 10.1108/K-07-2019-0469

[17] Peirce CS. Collected Papers of Charles Sanders Peirce. Vol. 1–8. Cambridge (MA): Harvard University Press; 1931–1958

[18] Lavanderos L. From cybersin to cybernet. Considerations for a cybernetics design thinking in the socialism of the XXI century. AI & SOCIETY. 2022;**37**:1279-1292. DOI: 10.1007/s00146-021-01354-2

[19] Lahitte HE, Hurrell JA, Malpartida A. Relations: From the Ecology of Ideas to the Idea of Ecology. Buenos Aires: Southern Hemisphere; 1987

[20] Bateson G. Mind and Nature: A Necessary Unity. New York: Dutton; 1979

[21] Lavanderos L, Malpartida A. Life as a relational unit, the process of ecopoiesis.

Kybernetes. 2023;**53**(12):5047-5060. DOI: 10.1108/K-05-2023-0859

[22] Malpartida AR. La noción de entorno en etología (una discusión etimo-epistemológica). Ecognición. 1991;**2**(1): 39-46

[23] Lavanderos L, Malpartida A. Cognición y territorio. In: Santiago de Chile: Comisión de Medio Ambiente y Bienes Nacionales del Senado de la República de Chile. Universidad Tecnológica Metropolitana; 2000. 110 p. Available from: https://www.academia.edu/75667653/Cognicion_y_Territorio

[24] Lavanderos L, Fiol E, Araya A. Assessing organizational cohesion by the maximum caliber method. Kybernetes. 2024. DOI: 10.1108/K-07-2024-1962

[25] Lavanderos L, Malpartida A. Relational theory of communication as an eco-semio-autopoietic process. Complexus. 2005;**1**(2):45-86. Available from: http://www.sintesys.cl/complexus/revista2/articulos2/complexus2.pdf

[26] Lavanderos L, Massey K. From Manufacturing to Mindfacture: A Relational Viable Systems Theory. Hershey (PA): IGI Global; 2015. 308 p. DOI: 10.4018/978-1-4666-7369-4

[27] Díaz-Barrera N, Lavanderos L. Beyond transdisciplinarity: Triferencial relational logic as an epistemic strategy for a complex and sustainable university. Frontiers in Education. 2025;**10**:1640472. DOI: 10.3389/feduc.2025.1640472

[28] Lavanderos L, Malpartida A. Relational theory of communication as an eco-semi-autopoietic process. Complexus. 2005;**1**(2):45-86. Available from: http://www.sintesys.cl/complexus/revista2/articulos2/complexus2.pdf

[29] Lavanderos L, Araya A, Malpartida A. Viability, sustainability, and non-requisite variety. Journal of Systemics, Cybernetics and Informatics. 2019;**17**(1):83-96

[30] Latour B. On actor-network theory: A few clarifications. Soziale Welt. 1996; **47**(4):369-381

[31] Malpartida A, Lavanderos L. Ecosystem and Ecotomo: A nature or society-nature relationship? Acta Biotheoretica. 2000;**48**(2):85-94. DOI: 10.1023/A:1002778625641

Chapter 4

# Edge AI for Smart Energy Systems: A Comprehensive Review

*Nguyen Anh Tuan and Ahn Yonghan*


## Abstract

This chapter reviews edge computing and artificial intelligence (AI) applications in digitalized energy infrastructures, addressing data processing challenges in smart grids and microgrids. By relocating analytics to field devices, Edge AI facilitates rapid decision-making and mitigates issues of bandwidth, privacy, and cybersecurity. The review examines edge-enabled solutions across five key domains: wide-area grid automation, microgrid and distributed energy resource management, demand response, electric vehicle charging networks, and predictive maintenance. Based on peer-reviewed studies and industry pilots, the analysis maps these applications to sustainability dimensions, including energy efficiency, cost-effectiveness, scalability, resilience, and emissions reduction. Findings indicate that edge solutions reduce control latency and upstream data traffic, defer network upgrades, and support increased renewable energy integration and demand-side flexibility, thereby lowering $CO_2$ emissions. The chapter also critically examines persistent challenges such as interoperability, hardware constraints, cyber-resilience, and large-scale orchestration, proposing a research agenda. Ultimately, Edge AI is presented as a crucial technology for a secure, low-carbon, and economically viable energy transition, contingent on addressing existing technical and institutional gaps.


**Keywords:** edge computing, edge AI, smart energy systems, sustainability, demand response

## 1. Introduction

Modern power systems are undergoing a digital transformation to accommodate the increasing penetration of renewable energy and distributed resources. The proliferation of Internet of Things (IoT) devices and advanced sensors in the grid has led to an explosion of data generation, straining traditional centralized computing approaches [1–3]. In parallel, the goals of the sustainable energy transition demand improvements in efficiency, reliability, affordability, and environmental performance. Latency, bandwidth costs, and privacy concerns increasingly constrain the ability of centralized platforms to deliver sub-second control actions that safeguard power quality and system stability.

Edge computing – processing data onsite or near the source – has emerged as a promising paradigm to meet these needs by reducing dependence on distant cloud data centers [2]. By bringing computation and intelligence closer to field devices, edge computing can dramatically cut latency, alleviate bandwidth bottlenecks, and enhance privacy and security [4, 5]. These benefits are crucial for smart energy systems such as smart grids, microgrids, and intelligent energy management, where real-time decision-making and local autonomy are increasingly important.

This review presents a comprehensive review of edge computing technologies – including edge artificial intelligence (Edge AI) – in the context of smart energy systems and the global renewable energy transition. No prior review, to our knowledge, has systematically synthesized the global body of evidence and linked it to a coherent sustainability framework that spans energy efficiency, cost-effectiveness, scalability-and-resilience, and emissions reduction. We explore how edge computing contributes to these four key sustainable development dimensions:

- Energy efficiency: optimizing energy generation, delivery, and consumption to minimize losses and waste.

- Cost-effectiveness: reducing operational and capital costs for utilities and consumers through smarter control and deferral of infrastructure upgrades.

- Scalability and resilience: enabling the energy system to reliably handle growth in connected devices and distributed resources and to withstand faults or disruptions.

- Emissions reduction and environmental impact: lowering greenhouse gas emissions and other environmental footprints by integrating renewables and improving system efficiency.

## 2. Edge computing in smart energy systems: Concepts and technologies

### 2.1 Defining edge AI in energy system context

Edge computing refers to a distributed computing paradigm that pushes data processing and analytics to the network edge – closer to sensors, actuators, and end-points – rather than relying solely on centralized cloud servers [6]. In energy systems, edge computing nodes can be located in substations, field devices (such as smart meters or protection relays), microgrid controllers, electric vehicle (EV) chargers, or even IoT gateways within homes and buildings. By processing data locally, edge nodes significantly reduce the volume of data that must be transmitted to the cloud, cutting communication costs and latency while improving data privacy [7, 8]. This is especially vital for power grids, where control actions (e.g., isolating a fault or regulating voltage) often need to be taken within milliseconds. Traditional cloud-based analysis can be too slow and bandwidth-intensive for such real-time requirements [9], whereas an edge-based approach enables immediate, onsite decision-making. **Table 1** describes the technological architecture components within Edge AI.

Edge AI in smart energy systems represents the deployment of artificial intelligence algorithms and machine learning models directly at network endpoints, field devices, and distributed infrastructure components rather than relying solely on centralized cloud computing resources [10]. This distributed computing paradigm fundamentally alters how energy systems process data, make decisions and execute control actions by bringing computational intelligence closer to the source of data

| Component | Role and Function | Key Technologies |
|---|---|---|
| Edge devices | Smart meters, relays, and EV chargers perform local data processing and immediate safety responses. Handles anomaly detection. | CUDA-accelerated GPUs |
| Fog layer | Substation/neighborhood-level analytics aggregating edge data. Manages pattern recognition and short-term forecasting. | Docker/Kubernetes |
| Cloud layer | Centralized oversight for long-term storage and strategic planning. Processes non-time-critical optimization tasks. | High-performance computing |
| Communication Infrastructure | Enables reliable data exchange between layers using 5G and optimized IoT protocols. Reduces backhaul bandwidth needs. | MQTT/CoAP |
| Virtualization Tools | Containerized deployment of analytics services across edge nodes. Enables remote updates and modular service scaling. | Docker/Kubernetes |
| Security Framework | Implements device authentication and encrypted data pipelines. Uses blockchain for secure edge transactions in pilots. | Federated learning |

**Table 1.**
*Technological architecture components.*

generation and the point of operational impact. In modern power grids, edge computing nodes are strategically positioned across the infrastructure ecosystem, including substations, smart meters, protection relays, microgrid controllers, electric vehicle charging stations, and even residential IoT gateways within homes and commercial buildings.

The architectural significance of this approach becomes apparent when considering the temporal requirements of power system operations. Traditional cloud-based analytics often introduce latency measured in hundreds of milliseconds or even seconds, which proves inadequate for critical grid control functions such as fault isolation, voltage regulation, and frequency stabilization that require response times measured in milliseconds [11]. Edge AI addresses this fundamental limitation by enabling immediate, onsite decision-making capabilities that can process sensor data, execute machine learning inference, and trigger prediction actions within the stringent timing requirements of electrical grid operations [12]. The technical implementation of Edge AI involves sophisticated lightweight neural networks and optimized algorithms specifically designed for resource-constrained environments. These systems utilize specialized hardware accelerators including Graphics Processing Units (GPUs), Tensor Processing Units (TPUs), and dedicated AI chips that enable complex machine learning computations on devices with limited power and computational resources [13].

## 2.2 Multi-tiered intelligence architecture

Contemporary smart energy systems employ hierarchical, multi-tiered architectures that strategically distribute intelligence across device, fog, and cloud layers to optimize both performance and cost-effectiveness [14]. At the device level, raw sensor data undergoes initial filtering and preprocessing using embedded controllers and microprocessors. This foundational layer handles basic threshold monitoring and immediate safety responses without requiring network connectivity [15].

The intermediate fog layer, typically implemented at substation or neighborhood levels, aggregates data from multiple edge devices and performs more sophisticated analytics [16]. This layer serves as a critical bridge between ultra-low-latency edge responses and comprehensive cloud-based optimization, enabling utilities to maintain both local autonomy and system-wide coordination [16].

The cloud layer provides global oversight, long-term data storage, complex optimization algorithms, and strategic planning capabilities while receiving only critical information and aggregated insights from the lower tiers [17]. This hierarchical approach creates a resilient infrastructure where each layer can continue operating even if connectivity to higher tiers is temporarily lost, ensuring continuous grid operation during communication disruptions or cyber incidents [17].

### 2.3 Enabling technologies and communication protocols

The successful deployment of Edge AI in energy systems depends on several key enabling technologies that facilitate efficient data exchange, virtualized service deployment, and robust cybersecurity. Modern communication protocols including Message Queuing Telemetry Transport (MQTT), Constrained Application Protocol (CoAP), and fifth-generation wireless technology (5G) enable efficient machine-to-machine data exchange with the low latency and high reliability required for grid applications [18].

Virtualization and containerization technologies, particularly Docker and Kubernetes platforms, allow utilities to deploy analytics services as lightweight, portable applications on edge hardware [19]. This approach enables rapid deployment of new algorithms, simplified maintenance, and the ability to update or modify edge intelligence without physical access to remote devices. The flexibility provided by containerized edge applications is particularly valuable for utilities managing geographically distributed infrastructure across diverse operating environments [19].

Cybersecurity mechanisms specifically designed for distributed edge environments include decentralized authentication protocols, end-to-end encryption, and distributed intrusion detection systems [20]. These security frameworks must address the unique challenges of protecting potentially millions of edge devices while maintaining the real-time performance requirements of grid operations [21].

## 3. Impact of edge computing in smart energy systems

Edge computing directly addresses several challenges of the evolving power system, translating into tangible benefits along the dimensions of efficiency, cost, resilience, and environmental impact. **Table 2** provides a synthesis of major edge computing applications in smart energy and their impacts on these key metrics. Below, we discuss each dimension in turn, highlighting mechanisms and examples through which edge computing contributes to sustainable energy goals.

### 3.1 Energy efficiency

By enabling faster and more granular control of energy flows, edge computing can significantly improve the energy efficiency of power generation, delivery, and end-use. Processing data locally allows for real-time optimizations that reduce waste and losses in the system. For instance, in microgrids with high renewable penetration,

| Edge application/ Use case | Energy Efficiency | Cost-Effectiveness | Resilience and Scalability | Emissions and Environmental |
|---|---|---|---|---|
| Wide-Area Smart Grid Control | Real-time voltage/frequency control reduces losses and improves power quality.<br>Faster fault detection minimizes energy wastage in faults. | Defers infrastructure upgrades by optimizing grid capacity use.<br>Lowers data backhaul costs by processing sensor data locally. | Localized control maintains stability during disturbances, preventing broad outages.<br>Easily scales: new feeders/devices managed by local edge nodes, not burdening central systems. | Enables higher integration of renewables through rapid balancing actions (more clean energy utilized).<br>Decreases the need for peaker plants by flattening peaks and cutting associated emissions. |
| Microgrids and DER Management | Optimizes onsite generation and storage use; minimizes curtailment of renewables.<br>Improves energy balance efficiency within the microgrid (less import/export losses). | Reduces energy purchase costs by maximizing cheap local solar/wind consumption.<br>Postpones grid upgrade costs by relieving strain through local supply-demand balancing. | Allows autonomous operation during grid outages (islanding), providing continuous power.<br>Scales modularly: new DER units come with local controllers that integrate into microgrid without central re-engineering. | Increases renewable penetration by managing variability in real time (more clean energy delivered).<br>Avoids diesel generator use through optimal dispatch, cutting local pollution and $CO_2$. |
| Demand Response & Smart Metering | Enhances end-use efficiency via immediate consumption feedback and device optimization.<br>Detects and reduces energy losses (e.g., theft or faults) through edge analytics on meter data. | Lowers consumer bills with dynamic pricing and load shifting (using edge to automate response).<br>Cuts utility peak capacity costs by shaving peaks at customer level. | Provides rapid demand relief in emergencies (edge controllers shed load to stabilize grid).<br>Highly scalable: millions of smart meters each handle local data, avoiding central bottlenecks. | Decreases reliance on peaking power plants by flattening demand spikes, reducing high-emission generation.<br>Facilitates distributed energy trading and prosumer participation, incentivizing renewables adoption. |
| EV Charging Networks | Aligns charging times with grid capacity, improving overall system efficiency (uses idle generation capacity effectively).<br>Reduces line congestion and associated losses by local load management at charging sites. | Avoids costly distribution upgrades by managing EV charging load within existing limits.<br>Lowers charging costs for consumers by scheduling when electricity is cheaper (edge decides optimal times). | Prevents localized overloads through real-time load control on chargers, enhancing grid reliability.<br>Scales to large EV fleets by distributed control – each station optimizes independently in coordination with grid signals. | Maximizes use of renewable energy for EVs by charging during renewable output periods.<br>Supports V2G services at edge (EVs feeding grid), displacing fossil backup generation and lowering overall emissions. |

| Edge application/ Use case | Energy Efficiency | Cost-Effectiveness | Resilience and Scalability | Emissions and Environmental |
|---|---|---|---|---|
| Predictive Maintenance and Asset Management | Keeps equipment at peak efficiency through continuous tuning and early issue correction.<br>Reduces energy waste from malfunctioning or degrading components (e.g., detecting a bad capacitor causing losses). | Saves maintenance costs by preventing catastrophic failures and optimizing crew dispatch.<br>Extends asset lifespan, deferring capital expenditure on replacements. | Cuts unplanned outages (up to 36% fewer) by predicting failures before they happen, improving system reliability.<br>Enhances safety by avoiding sudden equipment breakdowns that could cascade into larger disruptions. | Lowers emissions by ensuring generation assets run optimally (burning less fuel for the same output).<br>Avoids environmental incidents (like transformer oil leaks or fires) through early fault detection at the edge. |

**Table 2.**
*Edge computing applications in smart energy systems and their impact on key sustainability dimensions.*

edge-based controllers perform real-time forecasting of solar/wind generation and adjust battery charging or backup generators accordingly to avoid curtailment and ensure efficient use of available energy [22]. In a pilot microgrid in rural China, this kind of edge intelligence optimized generator dispatch and battery cycling in real time, minimizing energy spillage and improving the overall efficiency of the local energy usage [23]. Similarly, at the level of the broader smart grid, edge computing units in substations or along distribution feeders can dynamically balance loads and voltages. By reacting within milliseconds to fluctuations (e.g., through local voltage regulation or capacitor bank switching), these edge devices reduce resistive losses and prevent over-voltages, thus conserving energy that would otherwise be wasted as heat [24].

Edge computing also facilitates demand-side energy efficiency by processing consumption data from smart meters and IoT sensors to provide immediate feedback and control [25]. An edge-enabled home energy management system can analyze appliance usage patterns locally and perform on-the-fly optimizations such as turning off or throttling non-critical loads during peak times. One study demonstrated an IoT-based residential energy management approach with edge computing that used real-time data and reinforcement learning to shift loads and cut home energy costs, resulting in up to 20% improvement in user satisfaction while reducing peak demand [26]. This kind of automated demand response at the edge not only lowers bills but also translates to energy savings, since shifting or curtailing loads at peak times often avoids firing up inefficient peaking power plants.

Moreover, Edge AI enables predictive optimization – learning the operating patterns of equipment and finding efficiency gains. For example, edge devices running machine learning can perform non-intrusive load monitoring (NILM), disaggregating a building's total load to identify inefficient appliances or abnormal energy usage in near real time [27]. The presence of intelligence at the edge means these insights can trigger immediate corrective actions (like adjusting HVAC settings or notifying facility managers) rather than waiting for centralized analysis. In industrial settings, edge-based predictive control has been shown to fine-tune processes to save energy [28].

### 3.2 Cost-effectiveness and economic

Edge computing can improve cost-effectiveness for both utilities and consumers in multiple ways. First, by processing and filtering data locally, it reduces the volume of data transmitted to cloud centers, lowering communication infrastructure costs and cloud service expenditures. A comparative analysis of computing paradigms noted that edge computing results in dramatically lower data transmission and bandwidth usage than cloud-only approaches [29]. This translates into savings on backhaul communication costs, which can be significant given the massive scale of IoT data in modern grids. In advanced metering infrastructure (AMI) deployments, for example, millions of smart meters sending raw data to the cloud would impose high networking costs, whereas edge processing at neighborhood data concentrators or on meters themselves can compress and summarize data efficiently [30]. Kumari et al. [31] introduced a LoRa-based smart metering system with edge analytics that minimized data sent upstream and improved network efficiency.

More substantially, edge computing can defer or avoid costly infrastructure upgrades by optimizing the usage of existing assets. A salient case is in-home EV charging: Pacific Gas & Electric (PG&E) in California, together with Itron, launched a pilot where an edge computing application on the smart meter coordinates EV charging in real time [32]. This on-meter edge intelligence keeps the household's total load within safe limits, enabling homeowners with older 100-amp service panels to charge an EV at Level 2 speeds without upgrading to a costly 200-amp service [33]. By avoiding a panel and service upgrade (which can cost thousands of dollars), the edge solution delivers a direct economic benefit to consumers. At scale, such grid-edge management of EV and appliance loads can save utilities money as well, by reducing or delaying the need for distribution system reinforcements that would otherwise be required to handle growth in demand response [34].

Edge computing also enhances the cost-effectiveness of operations through improved reliability and maintenance practices (which have direct economic value). With edge-based monitoring and control, utilities can isolate faults faster and restore service more quickly after outages, thereby reducing outage durations and associated costs. For example, Florida Power & Light's deployment of smart sensors and edge analytics on its grid helped reduce outage duration by 25% and improved reliability indices by 20%, yielding significant operational savings [35]. Additionally, predictive maintenance empowered by Edge AI can cut maintenance costs by preventing catastrophic equipment failures and optimizing maintenance schedules. Duke Energy reported a 36% reduction in unplanned outages at its power plants by using edge analytics to detect equipment anomalies months in advance, translating to avoided downtime costs [36]. Such improvements typically offer a high return on investment – studies indicate predictive maintenance programs (which often rely on edge or onsite data processing for real-time insights) can deliver an ROI as high as 10:1 [37]. In summary, by reducing data handling costs, maximizing existing asset utilization, and lowering downtime and repair expenses, edge computing contributes to making smart energy systems more economically sustainable.

### 3.3 Scalability and system resilience

A decentralized edge computing approach inherently improves the scalability of smart energy systems. Instead of funneling all data and control through a central hub, intelligence distributed at the edge means the system can grow by adding more local nodes without overwhelming a single control center. Each edge node handles local tasks, so the computing load scales roughly with the number of nodes, not exponentially with data volume. Researchers have noted that edge computing "improves system scalability and availability" in smart grids, as new devices and data streams can be integrated with minimal incremental impact on latency or performance [38]. For instance, integrating thousands of rooftop solar systems and smart appliances is more feasible when using distributed edge controllers (such as local energy management systems) than if every sensor streamed data to a cloud that tries to manage them centrally. Distributed intelligence at the edge allows the overall system to accommodate a high density of DERs and IoT devices while maintaining real-time responsiveness [38]. Indeed, many utilities and grid operators view edge computing as essential to managing the growing complexity of the grid in a modular and scalable way [2].

Resilience – the ability of the energy system to withstand and quickly recover from disturbances – is markedly strengthened by edge computing. Because edge devices can continue to operate independently even if communication to the central cloud is lost or delayed, critical control functions can still be carried out locally during emergencies. This is crucial during cyber-attacks or natural disasters that might sever connectivity; microcontrollers at the edge (in microgrids, substations, etc.) can island sections of the grid and keep them running. Latency reduction is another key aspect: by eliminating the round-trip to a distant server, edge computing ensures that control actions (like tripping a breaker or adjusting frequency) occur with minimal delay, which can prevent cascading failures and equipment damage [24]. As a Schneider Electric analysis highlights, when smart grid devices require immediate responses for stability (e.g., frequency control in the final stage of power delivery), "placing edge computing power along the distributed substation networks mitigates latency and allows much faster control than relying on distant cloud servers" [24]. Faster local decision-making directly translates to greater grid stability under stress.

Edge computing enables autonomous microgrids and self-healing networks, which boost resilience [24]. In a microgrid, an edge controller can detect a grid outage and seamlessly transition the microgrid to islanded mode, coordinating local generators and storage to maintain power for critical loads. This was demonstrated in the aforementioned rural microgrid case, where an edge-based system maintained voltage and frequency stability in island mode via dynamic, intelligent control [39–41]. On the broader grid, distributed edge sensors and actuators (forming an intelligent mesh) can detect faults or disturbances and communicate with each other to reconfigure the network (by opening/closing switches) to isolate faults – a concept known as self-healing grids. Since the decision loop is local, these automatic reconfiguration actions happen in seconds, significantly reducing outage scope. Additionally, edge devices can continue performing critical security monitoring and protection functions if the cloud or control center is unreachable [42]. In short, decentralizing intelligence via edge computing improves both the robustness and flexibility of the energy system, ensuring it can scale to future demands and bounce back from adversities.

### 3.4 Emission reduction and environmental impact

Edge computing contributes to emissions reduction and environmental sustainability both directly and indirectly. One direct effect comes from the IT energy savings achieved by processing data efficiently at the edge. Large cloud data centers consume substantial electricity and contribute to carbon emissions (data centers account for ~2% of global $CO_2$ emissions) [43]. Edge computing, by performing computations onsite, reduces the need to continuously transmit data to central servers and thereby diminishes the workload on energy-hungry data centers [43]. In aggregate, a network of optimized edge devices can lower the overall ICT energy footprint. According to a sustainability analysis, "edge processing consumes much less energy than centralized infrastructure and can even reduce the need for power-hungry centralized data centers" [43]. Thus, adopting edge computing in IoT-heavy sectors like energy can curb the growth of emissions from the digital infrastructure itself.

More significantly, edge computing enables strategies that cut emissions in the operation of the energy system. By improving energy efficiency and grid optimization, as detailed in Section 3.1, edge-based control reduces losses and the unnecessary burning of fuel. Every kilowatt-hour saved through better voltage control or peak shaving translates to avoided generation, often from fossil-fueled plants. Demand response programs facilitated by edge devices are a clear example: when edge controllers in homes and buildings curtail or shift loads during peak periods, they help avoid calling on inefficient peaker plants (such as oil or gas turbines) that have high $CO_2$ per kWh. A study in Europe estimated that by 2020, demand response could lead to 100 TWh annual energy savings and ~ 30 million tons of $CO_2$ reduction [44]. Edge computing delivers such impacts by enabling faster and more reliable demand response at scale – devices can respond to grid signals or price changes instantaneously and in a coordinated manner without centralized intervention. IEA notes that digitalization (including smart edge devices) can automate demand response and harness distributed energy resources to reduce the need for new power plants and transmission lines, thereby avoiding emissions from construction and generation [34].

Another crucial area is the integration of renewable energy. Edge computing helps maximize the utilization of renewables by managing their variability locally. For example, intelligent edge controllers can perform emissions-aware optimizations, charging batteries or EVs when local solar/wind output is high (and clean) and delaying or reducing consumption when the grid is emitting more (e.g., during coal plant ramp-up). Smart EV charging algorithms implemented at the edge or charging station level can align charging times with periods of abundant renewable generation, which both reduces strain on the grid and cuts the carbon intensity of the electricity used by the EV [45]. A recent study found that smart charging and vehicle-to-grid (V2G) schemes could reduce overall energy system costs and increase investments in renewables, as flexible charging facilitates deeper penetration of wind and solar power [46]. In practice, this means an EV charging network with edge intelligence could soak up excess solar at midday or wind at night, instead of those clean electrons going to waste, thereby displacing fossil generation that would otherwise be needed at other times [47]. Edge computing is instrumental in these scenarios because decisions must be made based on local grid conditions and forecasts in real time (for instance, an edge device at a charging station deciding when to activate charging). By orchestrating loads and resources in an environmentally optimal way, edge intelligence directly supports emissions mitigation.

Finally, improved asset management *via* edge computing carries environmental benefits. Predictive maintenance avoids catastrophic failures like transformer blowouts or pipeline leaks that can cause environmental harm (oil spills, fires, etc.). It also extends the life of equipment, reducing the frequency of manufacturing and disposing of large electrical components – an often overlooked aspect of sustainability. Edge-based predictive maintenance keeps equipment operating at peak efficiency, which "reduces energy consumption and emissions while maintaining optimal output" [48, 49]. This implies, for example, that a gas turbine tuned via edge analytics will burn fuel more cleanly, or a wind farm with edge-monitored turbines will generate more electricity for the same wind (reducing the need for fossil backup). Thus, across multiple angles, edge computing serves as an enabler of greener outcomes in the power sector: it streamlines the digital footprint, and it unlocks advanced operational strategies that synergize with decarbonization objectives.

## 4. Technical challenges

### 4.1 Interoperability and standards development

The heterogeneous ecosystem of edge devices and platforms presents significant interoperability challenges that require coordinated standards development and industry collaboration. Different manufacturers utilize proprietary communication protocols, data formats, and system architectures that can impede seamless integration between devices from different vendors and across utility jurisdictions. The development of open standards and reference architectures for edge computing in power systems represents a critical priority for enabling plug-and-play device integration and coordinated system operation.

Current standardization efforts must address the complex requirements of distributed edge assets communicating with grid operators and coordinating with each other while maintaining the real-time performance requirements of electrical grid operations. This includes extending existing IoT and smart grid standards to accommodate the unique requirements of edge intelligence deployment at a utility scale. The challenge involves balancing standardization benefits with the need for innovation and technological differentiation among solution providers.

Successful interoperability frameworks must accommodate the multi-vendor, multi-technology environment that characterizes modern utility infrastructure while providing utilities with vendor-neutral approaches to edge intelligence deployment. This requires collaboration between utilities, technology vendors, standards organizations, and regulatory bodies to develop comprehensive frameworks that address technical, operational, and cybersecurity requirements.

### 4.2 Resource constraints and edge device optimization

Edge devices often operate under severe resource constraints including limited computational power, memory capacity, and energy supply, particularly for remote or battery-powered sensors. Running advanced AI algorithms on these resource-constrained platforms requires significant optimization of both hardware and software components. Research into energy-efficient edge processors and adaptive algorithms specifically designed for utility applications represents a critical area for continued development.

Techniques such as model compression, quantization, and edge-friendly machine learning (tinyML) enable the deployment of sophisticated AI capabilities on devices with limited computational resources. These methods must balance algorithmic sophistication with the practical limits of field-deployed hardware, while maintaining the accuracy and reliability required for critical grid operations demand. Dynamic task allocation between edge and cloud computing resources provides another approach to optimize performance by ensuring that time-critical functions remain at the edge while computationally intensive analytics can be performed in the cloud when connectivity allows.

The development of specialized hardware accelerators and AI chips designed specifically for utility edge applications offers promising opportunities to enhance computational capabilities while minimizing power consumption. These custom solutions must address the unique environmental and operational requirements of utility infrastructure, including extended temperature ranges, electromagnetic interference, and long operational lifespans measured in decades rather than years.

### 4.3 Cybersecurity and data privacy frameworks

The distributed nature of Edge AI deployments significantly expands the attack surface for cyber threats, with each edge node potentially serving as an entry point for malicious actors. Ensuring robust security for potentially millions of edge devices requires innovative approaches to authentication, encryption, and intrusion detection that can operate effectively in resource-constrained environments. Lightweight yet strong encryption schemes and decentralized authentication mechanisms represent active areas of research with direct applicability to utility-edge deployments.

Blockchain and distributed ledger technologies have been proposed as potential solutions for securing edge transactions and device coordination, but their practicality and scalability in real grid environments require further evaluation. These technologies must demonstrate the ability to provide security benefits while meeting the stringent performance requirements of electrical grid operations. Privacy considerations become particularly important when edge devices handle sensitive customer data from smart meters and home energy management systems.

Federated learning approaches that enable AI model training across distributed edge devices while keeping personal data local represent promising solutions for balancing analytics capabilities with privacy requirements. These frameworks must address the technical challenges of coordinating machine learning across heterogeneous devices while maintaining data privacy and system security.

### 4.4 Scalable edge management and orchestration

Managing vast distributed networks of edge computing nodes presents significant operational challenges that require new approaches to device monitoring, software deployment, and resource orchestration. Utilities need automated management frameworks that can treat large fleets of edge devices as coordinated, scalable resources while maintaining individual device functionality and reliability. This includes developing optimal strategies for placing services and microservices between cloud and edge computing resources to meet latency requirements while minimizing operational costs.

Edge-fog-cloud collaboration strategies require sophisticated coordination mechanisms that can automatically determine which data and decisions should propagate upward versus remaining localized for optimal grid performance. AI-driven coordination schemes may provide solutions for these complex optimization problems, but they must demonstrate reliability and predictability in mission-critical utility environments. The challenge involves balancing local autonomy with system-wide optimization while maintaining real-time performance requirements.

Automated orchestration frameworks must address the unique requirements of utility infrastructure, including geographic distribution, environmental challenges, and regulatory compliance requirements. These systems must provide utilities with comprehensive visibility and control over their edge computing infrastructure while minimizing manual intervention and operational complexity.

### 4.5 Advanced real-time analytics and distributed AI

Current edge implementations often utilize relatively simple control logic and threshold-based algorithms, representing only a fraction of the potential capabilities of sophisticated Edge AI systems. Fully leveraging edge computing will require the deployment of more advanced real-time analytics and AI algorithms capable of autonomous grid reconfiguration, adaptive control under uncertainty, and cooperative learning among distributed edge devices. Multi-agent systems deployed at the edge offer promising approaches for enabling devices or subsystems to negotiate and collaborate toward global optimization objectives.

Research into multi-agent deep reinforcement learning at the edge shows promise for managing microgrids and distribution networks, but translating these academic developments to field deployment remains a significant challenge. Ensuring that AI methods remain reliable and explainable in mission-critical grid operations represents a fundamental requirement that must be addressed before widespread deployment of advanced edge intelligence. The utility industry's emphasis on safety and reliability requires that AI systems demonstrate predictable behavior and provide operators with sufficient visibility into decision-making processes.

Cooperative learning frameworks that enable edge devices to share insights and improve performance through distributed machine learning represent an emerging frontier with significant potential benefits. These systems must address the challenges of coordinating learning across devices with different capabilities, operating in diverse environments, and serving various grid functions while maintaining overall system stability and performance.

## 5. Future research and conclusions

### 5.1 Validation and pilot project requirements

The advancement of Edge AI in energy systems requires comprehensive real-world pilot projects and longitudinal studies to quantify benefits across diverse operational scenarios and grid conditions. While numerous simulations and limited case studies suggest improvements in latency, efficiency, and cost-effectiveness, utilities require clearer business cases with quantified return on investment metrics before committing to large-scale deployments. Areas requiring additional validation include comprehensive cost-benefit analysis, carbon accounting for edge implementations, and long-term reliability assessment of edge devices under utility operating conditions.

Global collaboration on pilot deployments across both developed and developing power systems can provide critical insights into how Edge AI performs under different grid architectures, regulatory environments, and scales of deployment. These pilots should address the unique challenges of various grid modernization contexts, from advanced smart grid implementations in developed countries to foundational electrification efforts in emerging economies. Such comprehensive testing will help refine both technical specifications and regulatory frameworks needed to support widespread Edge AI adoption.

Pilot projects must also address integration challenges with existing utility infrastructure, including legacy systems that may lack modern communication capabilities or standardized interfaces. The development of migration strategies that enable utilities to incrementally deploy Edge AI capabilities while maintaining compatibility with existing investments represents a critical area for practical research and development.

### 5.2 Regulatory framework development

The proliferation of Edge AI in energy systems will require updated regulatory frameworks that accommodate distributed intelligence while maintaining grid safety and reliability standards. Current protection standards and operational procedures may need revision to allow for distributed control actions and autonomous decision-making by edge devices. Regulatory bodies must balance innovation enablement with risk management, ensuring that new technologies enhance rather than compromise grid stability and public safety.

Tariff structures and incentive mechanisms require development to appropriately value the grid services provided by Edge AI systems and encourage customer participation in edge-driven demand response programs. These economic frameworks must recognize the benefits of distributed intelligence while ensuring fair cost allocation among utility customers. Market designs for distributed energy resources must evolve to accommodate the capabilities of Edge AI for coordinating complex interactions between generation, storage, and flexible loads.

Data governance and privacy regulations must address the unique characteristics of edge computing deployments, particularly regarding customer data handling and cross-jurisdictional data flows. Regulatory frameworks must provide clear guidance on data ownership, sharing, and protection requirements while enabling the data analytics capabilities that make Edge AI valuable for grid operations.

### 5.3 Integration with emerging technologies

The successful implementation of Edge AI in energy systems requires significant workforce development and organizational transformation within utility companies. Traditional utility operations personnel must develop new skills in data analytics, AI system management, and edge computing technologies while maintaining their expertise in electrical engineering and grid operations. Training programs must address both technical competencies and the cultural change required to leverage distributed intelligence effectively.

Organizational structures within utilities may need to evolve to support Edge AI operations, including new roles for data scientists, AI specialists, and edge computing engineers. The integration of these new capabilities with traditional grid operations requires careful coordination to ensure that Edge AI enhances rather than disrupts established safety and reliability procedures. Change management strategies must address the concerns of experienced utility personnel while building confidence in new technologies.

Collaboration among utilities, universities, and technology providers will be essential for developing the workforce capabilities needed to support widespread Edge AI deployment. Educational programs must evolve to include Edge AI concepts in traditional power systems curricula while providing continuing education opportunities for current utility professionals. Industry certification programs for Edge AI in energy systems could help standardize competency requirements and facilitate workforce mobility across utility organizations.

### 5.4 Workforce development and organizational change

The successful implementation of Edge AI in energy systems requires significant workforce development and organizational transformation within utility companies. Traditional utility operations personnel must develop new skills in data analytics, AI system management, and edge computing technologies while maintaining their expertise in electrical engineering and grid operations. Training programs must address both technical competencies and the cultural change required to leverage distributed intelligence effectively.

Organizational structures within utilities may need to evolve to support Edge AI operations, including new roles for data scientists, AI specialists, and edge computing engineers. The integration of these new capabilities with traditional grid operations requires careful coordination to ensure that Edge AI enhances rather than disrupts established safety and reliability procedures. Change management strategies must address the concerns of experienced utility personnel while building confidence in new technologies.

Collaboration between utilities, universities, and technology providers will be essential for developing the workforce capabilities needed to support widespread Edge AI deployment. Educational programs must evolve to include Edge AI concepts in traditional power systems curricula while providing continuing education opportunities for current utility professionals. Industry certification programs for Edge AI in energy systems could help standardize competency requirements and facilitate workforce mobility across utility organizations.

## 6. Conclusion

Edge AI represents a transformative technology that is fundamentally reshaping the architecture, operation, and capabilities of modern energy systems. Through the strategic deployment of artificial intelligence at network endpoints and field devices, utilities are achieving unprecedented levels of operational efficiency, cost reduction, and environmental performance while enhancing system resilience and scalability. The comprehensive review presented in this chapter demonstrates that Edge AI delivers quantifiable benefits across all critical dimensions of sustainable energy system operation: energy efficiency improvements through real-time optimization, substantial cost reductions through infrastructure deferment and operational improvements, enhanced scalability and resilience through distributed intelligence, and significant emissions reductions through improved renewable energy integration and system optimization.

The technical maturity demonstrated by current implementations, from PG&E's innovative EV charging solutions to FPL's comprehensive grid monitoring systems and Duke Energy's predictive maintenance programs, validates the practical viability of Edge AI for utility-scale deployment.

However, the full potential of Edge AI in energy systems remains constrained by several technical and institutional challenges that require coordinated research and development efforts. Interoperability standards must evolve to accommodate heterogeneous edge device ecosystems while maintaining the real-time performance requirements of electrical grid operations. Resource constraints in edge devices necessitate continued advancement in energy-efficient processing hardware and optimized AI algorithms specifically designed for utility applications. Cybersecurity frameworks must address the expanded attack surface created by distributed edge deployments while maintaining the stringent reliability requirements of critical infrastructure.

The path forward requires sustained collaboration between utilities, technology providers, regulatory bodies, and research institutions to address these challenges while advancing the state of the art in Edge AI capabilities. Comprehensive pilot projects across diverse grid architectures and operating environments will provide the validation and quantification needed to build utility confidence in large-scale Edge AI deployment. Regulatory frameworks must evolve to accommodate distributed intelligence while maintaining safety and reliability standards, and workforce development programs must prepare utility personnel for the operational transformation enabled by Edge AI technologies.

Looking toward the future, Edge AI will serve as a foundational technology enabling the next generation of smart energy systems characterized by autonomous operation, predictive optimization, and seamless integration of distributed energy resources. The convergence of Edge AI with emerging technologies including 5G communications, blockchain, and advanced energy storage will create new opportunities for innovation and performance improvement. As the global energy sector continues its transition toward renewable resources and electrified transportation, Edge AI will provide the intelligent infrastructure needed to manage complexity, optimize performance, and ensure reliable operation at unprecedented scales.

## Acknowledgements

This work was supported by the National Research Foundation of Korea(NRF) grant funded by the Korea government(MSIT) (No. RS-2023-00217322).

## Author details

Nguyen Anh Tuan[1*] and Ahn Yonghan[2]

1 Department of Smart City Engineering, Hanyang University ERICA Campus, Ansan, Gyeonggi-do, Republic of Korea

2 Department of Architecture Engineering, Hanyang University ERICA Campus, Ansan, Gyeonggi-do, Republic of Korea

*Address all correspondence to: natuan@hanyang.ac.kr

## References

[1] Sharma M, Tomar A, Hazra A. Edge computing for industry 5.0: Fundamental, applications, and research challenges. IEEE Internet of Things Journal. 1 Jun 2024;**11**(11):19070-19093. DOI: 10.1109/JIOT.2024.3359297

[2] Yıldırım F, Yalman Y, Bayındır KÇ, Terciyanlı E. Comprehensive review of edge computing for power systems: State of the art, architecture, and applications. Applied Sciences. 2025;**15**(8):4592. DOI: 10.3390/app15084592

[3] Liang S, Jin S, Chen Y. A review of edge computing technology and its applications in power systems. Energies. 2024;**17**(13):3230

[4] Jiang C, Cheng X, Gao H, Zhou X, Wan J. Toward computation offloading in edge computing: A survey. IEEE Access. 2019;7:131543-131558

[5] Nain G, Pattanaik K, Sharma G. Towards edge computing in intelligent manufacturing: Past, present and future. Journal of Manufacturing Systems. 2022;**62**:588-611

[6] Buyya R, Srirama SN, editors. Fog and Edge Computing: Principles and Paradigms. John Wiley & Sons; 2019

[7] Zhang J, Chen B, Zhao Y, Cheng X, Hu F. Data security and privacy-preserving in edge computing paradigm: Survey and open issues. IEEE Access. 2018;**6**:18209-18237

[8] El-Sayed H et al. Edge of things: The big picture on the integration of edge, IoT and the cloud in a distributed computing environment. IEEE Access. 2017;**6**:1706-1717

[9] Bilal K, Khalid O, Erbad A, Khan SU. Potentials, trends, and prospects in edge technologies: Fog, cloudlet, mobile edge, and micro data centers. Computer Networks. 2018;**130**:94-120

[10] Duan S et al. Distributed artificial intelligence empowered by end-edge-cloud computing: A survey. IEEE Communications Surveys and Tutorials. 2022;**25**(1):591-624

[11] Zhao Z, Yang P, Guerrero JM, Xu Z, Green TC. Multiple-time-scales hierarchical frequency stability control strategy of medium-voltage isolated microgrid. IEEE Transactions on Power Electronics. 2015;**31**(8):5974-5991

[12] Gooi HB, Wang T, Tang Y. Edge intelligence for smart grid: A survey on application potentials. CSEE Journal of Power and Energy Systems. 2023;**9**(5):1623-1640

[13] Chang Z, Liu S, Xiong X, Cai Z, Tu G. A survey of recent advances in edge-computing-powered artificial intelligence of things. IEEE Internet of Things Journal. 2021;**8**(18):13849-13875

[14] Hashem IA, Siddiqa A, Alaba FA, Bilal M, Alhashmi SM. Distributed intelligence for IoT-based smart cities: A survey. Neural Computing and Applications. 2024;**36**(27):16621-16656

[15] Yu W et al. A survey on the edge computing for the internet of things. IEEE Access. 2017;**6**:6900-6919

[16] Mouradian C, Naboulsi D, Yangui S, Glitho RH, Morrow MJ, Polakos PA. A comprehensive survey on fog computing: State-of-the-art and research challenges. IEEE Communications Surveys and Tutorials. 2017;**20**(1):416-464

[17] Osanaiye O, Chen S, Yan Z, Lu R, Choo K-KR, Dlodlo M. From cloud to fog computing: A review and a conceptual live VM migration framework. IEEE Access. 2017;**5**:8284-8300

[18] Akpakwu GA, Mathonsi TE, Tshilongamulenze TM, Maswikaneng SP, Muchenje T. Congestion Control in Constrained Application Protocol for the Internet of Things: State-of-the-Art, Challenges and Future Directions. IEEE Access; 2025

[19] Bentaleb O, Belloum AS, Sebaa A, El-Maouhab A. Containerization technologies: Taxonomies, applications and challenges. The Journal of Supercomputing. 2022;**78**(1):1144-1181

[20] Sha K, Yang TA, Wei W, Davari S. A survey of edge computing-based designs for IoT security. Digital Communications and Networks. 2020;**6**(2):195-202

[21] Molokomme DN, Onumanyi AJ, Abu-Mahfouz AM. Edge intelligence in smart grids: A survey on architectures, offloading models, cyber security measures, and challenges. Journal of Sensor and Actuator Networks. 2022;**11**(3):47

[22] Asit Kumar Majhi A, Mohanty S. A comprehensive review on internet of things applications in power systems. IEEE Internet of Things Journal. 1 Nov 2024;**11**(21):34896-34923. DOI: 10.1109/JIOT.2024.3447241

[23] Hong G, Hanjing C. An edge computing architecture and application oriented to distributed microgrid. In: 2021 IEEE Intl Conf on Parallel & Distributed Processing with Applications, Big Data & Cloud Computing, Sustainable Computing & Communications, Social Computing & Networking (ISPA/BDCloud/SocialCom/SustainCom). New York City, NY, USA; 2021. pp. 611-617. DOI: 10.1109/ISPA-BDCloud-SocialCom-SustainCom52081.2021.00089

[24] Daccach E. How Edge Computing Is Driving Smart Grid Responsiveness and Resilience. 8 Nov 2022. Available from: https://blog.se.com/infrastructure-and-grid/smart-grid/2022/11/08/how-edge-computing-driving-smart-grid-responsiveness-resilience/ [Accessed 2025]

[25] Cicirelli F, Gentile AF, Greco E, Guerrieri A, Spezzano G, Vinci A. An energy management system at the edge based on reinforcement learning. In: 2020 IEEE/ACM 24th International Symposium on Distributed Simulation and Real Time Applications (DS-RT). Prague, Czech Republic; 2020. pp. 1-8. DOI: 10.1109/DS-RT50469.2020.9213697

[26] Ruan L, Yan Y, Guo S, Wen F, Qiu X. Priority-based residential energy management with collaborative edge and cloud computing. IEEE Transactions on Industrial Informatics. 2019;**16**(3):1848-1857

[27] Hudson N, Hossain MJ, Hosseinzadeh M, Khamfroush H, Rahnamay-Naeini M, Ghani N. A framework for edge intelligent smart distribution grids via federated learning. In: 2021 International Conference on Computer Communications and Networks (ICCCN). Athens, Greece; 2021. pp. 1-9. DOI: 10.1109/ICCCN52240.2021.9522360

[28] Molokomme DN, Chabalala CS, Bokoro PN. A review of cognitive radio smart grid communication infrastructure systems. Energies. 2020;**13**(12):3245

[29] Andriulo FC, Fiore M, Mongiello M, Traversa E, Zizzo V. Edge computing and cloud computing for internet of things: A

review. Informatics. 2024;**11**(4):71. DOI: 10.3390/informatics11040071

[30] Al-Turjman F, Abujubbeh M. IoT-enabled smart grid via SM: An overview. Future Generation Computer Systems. 2019;**96**:579-590

[31] Kumari P, Mishra R, Gupta HP, Dutta T, Das SK. An energy efficient smart metering system using edge computing in LoRa network. IEEE Transactions on Sustainable Computing. 2021;7(4):786-798

[32] Intersolar. Itron, PG&E Announce Real-Time Control EV Charging Pilot Program with Grid Edge Intelligence. 14 Nov 2024. Available from: https://www.intersolar.us/news-insights/ev-charging-infrastructure/itron-pge-announce-real-time-control-ev-charging-pilot-program-with-grid-edge-intelligence/ [Accessed 2025]

[33] P. G. a. E. Company. Itron and PG&E Collaborate to Enable Real-Time Control of Electric Vehicle Charging with Grid Edge Intelligence. 13 Nov 2024. Available from: https://www.prnewswire.com/news-releases/itron-and-pge-collaborate-to-enable-real-time-control-of-electric-vehicle-charging-with-grid-edge-intelligence-302304572.html [Accessed 2025]

[34] IEA. Demand Response. 2025. Available from: https://www.iea.org/energy-system/energy-efficiency-and-demand/demand-response [Accessed 2025]

[35] U.S. Department of Energy. Office of Electricity, 2020 Smart Grid System Report. Washington, DC, USA; Jan 2022. Available from: https://www.energy.gov/sites/default/files/2022-05/2020%20Smart%20Grid%20System%20Report_0.pdf

[36] Energy D. Annual Sustainability Report. 2019. Available from: https://sustainabilityreport.duke-energy.com/

[37] Deloitte. Predictive Maintenance and the Smart Factory. 2021. Available from: https://www2.deloitte.com/content/dam/Deloitte/us/Documents/process-and-operations/us-cons-predictive-maintenance.pdf

[38] Feng C, Wang Y, Chen Q, Ding Y, Strbac G, Kang C. Smart grid encounters edge computing: Opportunities and applications. Advances in Applied Energy. 2021;**1**:100006

[39] Dong W, Yang Q, Li W, Zomaya AY. Machine-learning-based real-time economic dispatch in islanding microgrids in a cloud-edge computing environment. IEEE Internet of Things Journal. 2021;**8**(17):13703-13711

[40] Chen S et al. Internet of things based smart grids supported by intelligent edge computing. IEEE Access. 2019;**7**:74089-74102

[41] Lv L, Wu Z, Zhang L, Gupta BB, Tian Z. An edge-AI based forecasting approach for improving smart microgrid efficiency. IEEE Transactions on Industrial Informatics. 2022;**18**(11):7946-7954

[42] Zeng P, Liang H, Zhang N, Song C. Recent advances of edge computing for smart grid. Frontiers in Energy Research. 2023;**11**:1229000

[43] Locke J. How Edge Computing Supports Sustainability. 27 Jun 2024. Available from: https://www.digi.com/blog/post/how-edge-computing-supports-sustainability [Accessed]

[44] Sousa J, Soares I. The effect of demand response on $CO_2$ emissions in the Iberian electricity market–combining

economic and environmental perspectives. Energy and Climate Change. 2023;**4**:100093

[45] Heinisch V, Göransson L, Erlandsson R, Hodel H, Johnsson F, Odenberger M. Smart electric vehicle charging strategies for sectoral coupling in a city energy system. Applied Energy. 2021;**288**:116640

[46] Bogdanov D, Breyer C. Role of smart charging of electric vehicles and vehicle-to-grid in integrated renewables-based energy systems on country level. Energy. 2024;**301**:131635

[47] Lewis C, Bronski P, McCormick G, Amuchastegui N. How Emissions-Optimized EV Charging Enables Cleaner Electric Vehicles. Tech. Rep. Oakland, CA, USA: WattTime; Sep 2019. [Online]. Available from: https://watttime.org/wp-content/uploads/2024/01/WattTime-EVAnalysis-FullReport-vFinal.pdf [Accessed: 2025]

[48] Hafeez T, Xu L, Mcardle G. Edge intelligence for data handling and predictive maintenance in IIOT. IEEE Access. 2021;**9**:49355-49371

[49] Artiushenko V et al. Resource-efficient Edge AI solution for predictive maintenance. Procedia Computer Science. 2024;**232**:348-357

Chapter 5

# Observability and Auding in a Scalable Multi-Tenant Distributed Systems

*Rajasrikar Punugoti and Sirisha Manam*


## Abstract

Observability and auditing is critical in distributed architectures, as it allows for the observation of each service's interactions with other services and the ecosystem, enabling the understanding of incidents and the identification of patterns and trends. In the world of scalable multi-tenant distributed architecture, observability provides greater operational insight, enabling the detection of anomalies and the troubleshooting of issues. Observability refers to the ability to monitor and understand the behavior and performance of systems made up of different software programming languages. The article proposes how to build tools to collecting, storing, and analyzing data to enable the identification of patterns and trends, as well as the troubleshooting of issues to improve Observability and Auditing.


**Keywords:** observability, auditing, distributed systems, tracing, multi-tenancy

## 1. Introduction

Observability is about collecting critical telemetry data with relevant context and using that data to quickly determine your systems' behavior and health. This capability is crucial in today's fast-paced, microservices-driven, distributed environments, where the complexity and dynamic nature of systems demand robust and flexible observability solutions.

With monitoring, you track items but must infer why something occurred or how it is related to another event. With observability, you use information to prove facts and use that knowledge to determine how or why something behaves the way it does.

To provide monitoring, either your application needs to be instrumented to emit health data or you are required to infer the health of the application by watching its external behavior [1]. In either case, the data collected needs to be able to track and answer questions about availability, performance, and security.

Observability in multi-tenancy distributed microservice systems refers to the ability to monitor and understand the behavior and performance of a system made up of microservices, enabling the identification of patterns, trends, and incidents.



IntechOpen

## 2. Importance of observability in a multi-tenant polyglot systems

Implementing observability patterns, such as health checks, log aggregation, and distributed tracing, is essential for designing production-ready services. These patterns provide insight into application behavior, enabling the understanding of runtime behavior and the troubleshooting of problems. Observability is vital to have metrics, tracing, logging, visualization, and alerting capabilities for all processes, services, and components [2]. As explains, in a multi-tenant distributed architecture style, where each service runs in its own process, allowing for extreme decoupling and scalability. However, this also introduces additional complexity, making observability even more critical.

### 2.1 Multi tenancy

Multi-tenancy is a mode of operation in which a single application that is responsible for supporting multiple distinct independent customers or users.

(tenants) operate in a shared environment. In a multi-tenant environment, multiple customers are utilizing the same application resources [hardware and software] at the same time, which is the main business model for public cloud providers.

The aim of using multi-tenancy in cloud computing is to provide a shared environment where multiple tenants can coexist without compromising the security and integrity of each other's data [3].

Multi-tenancy is a widely used architectural pattern for building SaaS systems, where multiple tenants share the same hardware and software resources. This approach provides several benefits, including reduced costs, increased scalability, and improved resource utilization. In a multi-tenant system, each tenant has its own users, roles, and permissions, and resources are isolated between tenants (**Figure 1**).

### 2.2 Polyglot systems

Polyglot systems in distributed architecture refer to the ability of each microservice to be implemented in a different programming language or technology stack, allowing for

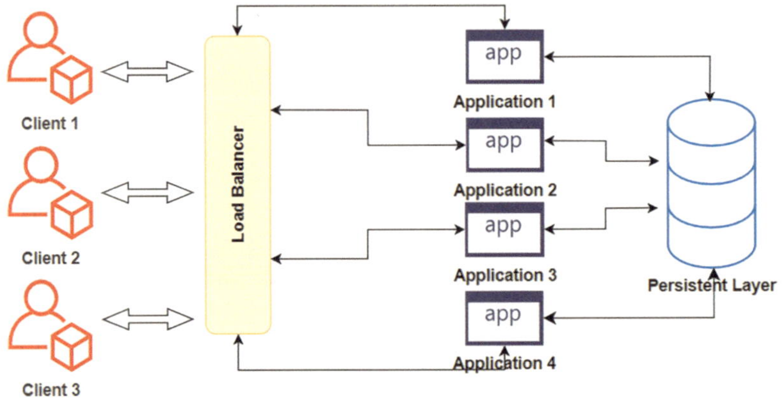


**Figure 1.**
*Multi-tenant architecture.*

greater flexibility and autonomy. Polyglot systems are designed to give developers the freedom to choose the best language or technology [4] for each microservice, rather than being restricted to a single language or technology stack. The benefits of polyglot systems include increased flexibility, autonomy, and scalability. Each microservice can be developed, tested, and deployed independently, without affecting other services.

However, polyglot systems also introduce new challenges, such as increased complexity, security risks, and communication overhead. Each microservice must be designed to communicate with other services, which can be challenging, especially when using different languages or technologies.

To implement polyglot systems effectively, developers should follow best practices such as using APIs and messaging systems to communicate between services. Each microservice should be designed to be autonomous and independent, with its own database and security mechanisms. Developers should also use containerization and orchestration tools, such as Docker and Kubernetes, to manage and deploy polyglot systems (**Figure 2**).

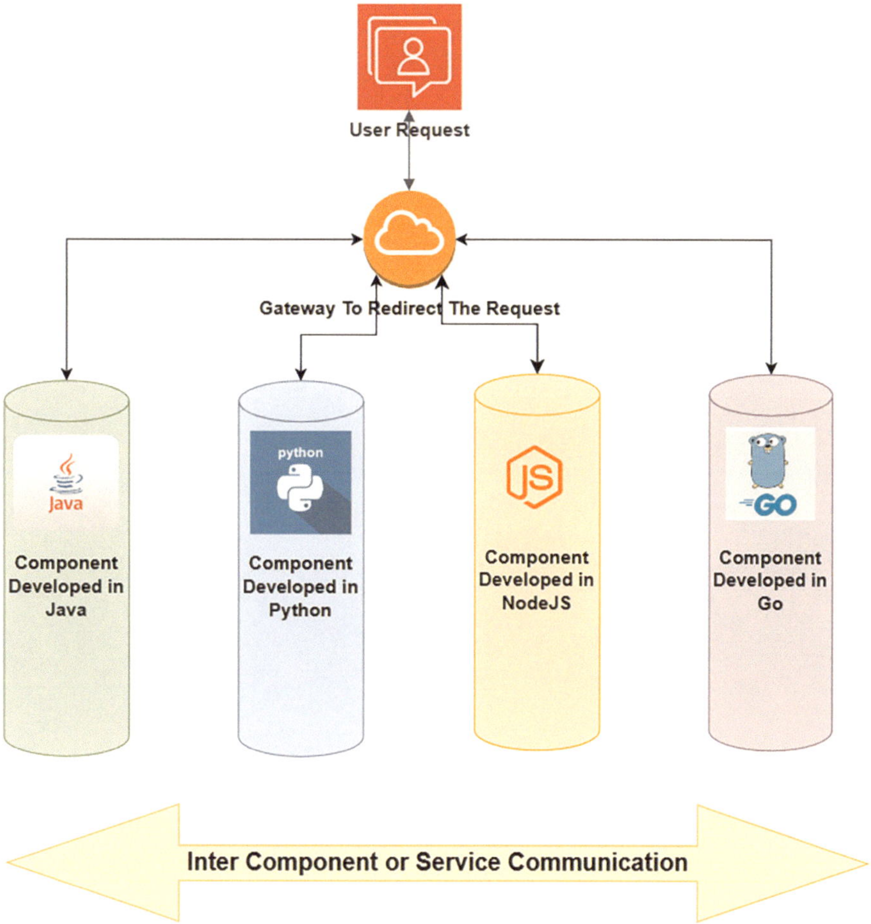


**Figure 2.**
*Polyglot systems.*

## 2.3 Distributed system considerations

Distributed systems are a collection of individual systems that work together to support a resource or provide a service. It is designed to support communication and coordination among its members to achieve a common function, goal, or operation.

There are various types of distributed systems, including client–server architectures, peer-to-peer architectures, and distributed computing environments. Client–server architectures are commonly used in web applications, where a client requests resources from a server. Peer-to-peer architectures, on the other hand, enable distributed sharing of responsibilities, duties, resources without a central location.

Distributed systems [5] have several advantages, such as heterogeneity of components, service interdependencies, scalability, reliability, and performance. However, they also pose Latency, error handling, can complicate the task of collecting, correlating, and analyzing telemetry data. To address these challenges, it is essential to use tools and techniques that can handle the complexity of distributed systems, such as Open Telemetry [2] and Observability (**Figure 3**).

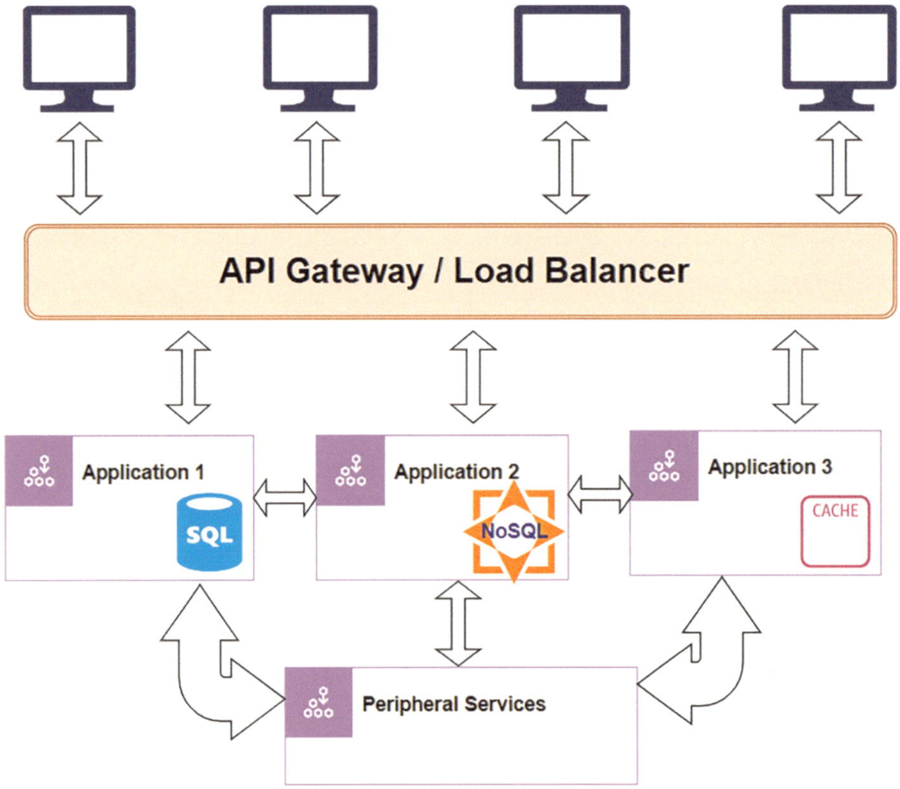


**Figure 3.**
*Distributed architecture.*

## 2.4 Containers

A container in service architecture is a standard unit of software that is lightweight and portable units that package an application code, runtime, libraries and its dependencies, allowing the application for consistent deployment across different environments to run quickly and reliably from one computing environment to another [6].

The container architecture is designed to provide a high degree of availability and scalability. It is divided into two parts: the container and the image. The container is managed by the Container service, and the image is created for building new services.

An example of containerization can be seen in the use of Docker, which provides a lightweight way to provision isolated execution for service instances. Docker uses a Dockerfile to build a Docker image, which can then be used to create a container. The Docker image is immutable, and the container can be run on any infrastructure, making it a popular choice for deploying microservices (**Figure 4**).

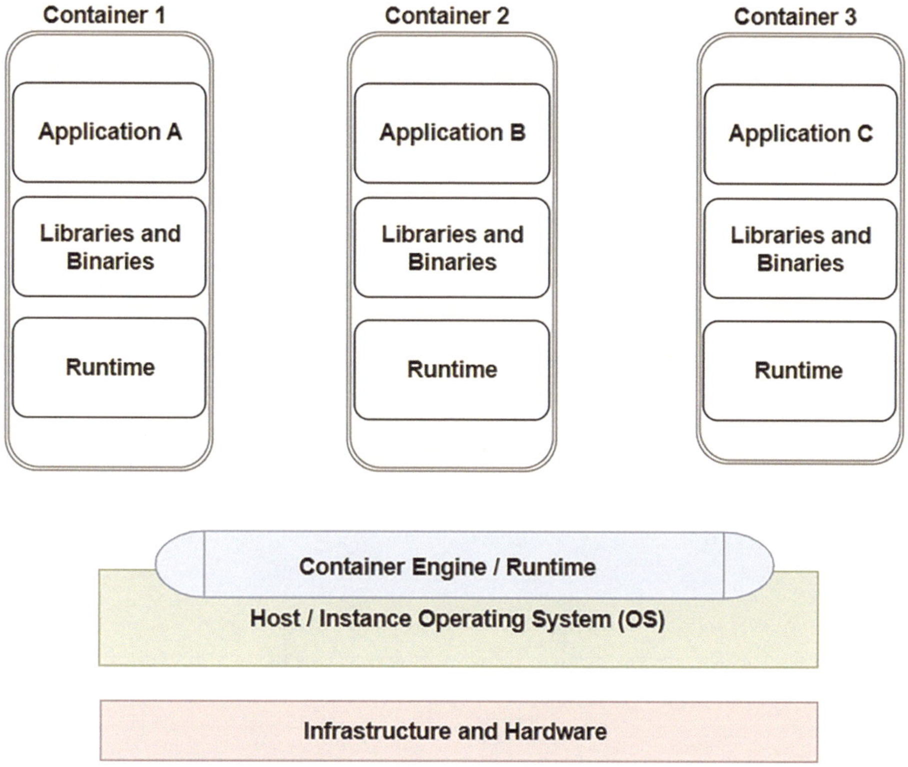


**Figure 4.**
*Container environment / service.*

### 2.5 Sidecar

A sidecar is a secondary container that runs alongside a primary service container, providing additional services such as monitoring, logging, and configuration [7].

Sidecar systems in observability are used to collect and export metrics, logs, and tracing data from microservices applications, providing valuable insights into the provides visibility over the application's traffic, system's performance, and health.

The use of sidecar systems provides several benefits, including automated instrumentation of applications, which simplifies the process of monitoring and logging. Additionally, sidecar systems can inject errors into transactions to test the system's resilience and observability. This allows developers to identify and fix issues before they become critical.

The implementation of sidecar systems typically involves deploying a sidecar container alongside the application container in the same pod. This sidecar container can be configured to collect and export metrics, logs, and tracing data to a centralized monitoring system (**Figure 5**).

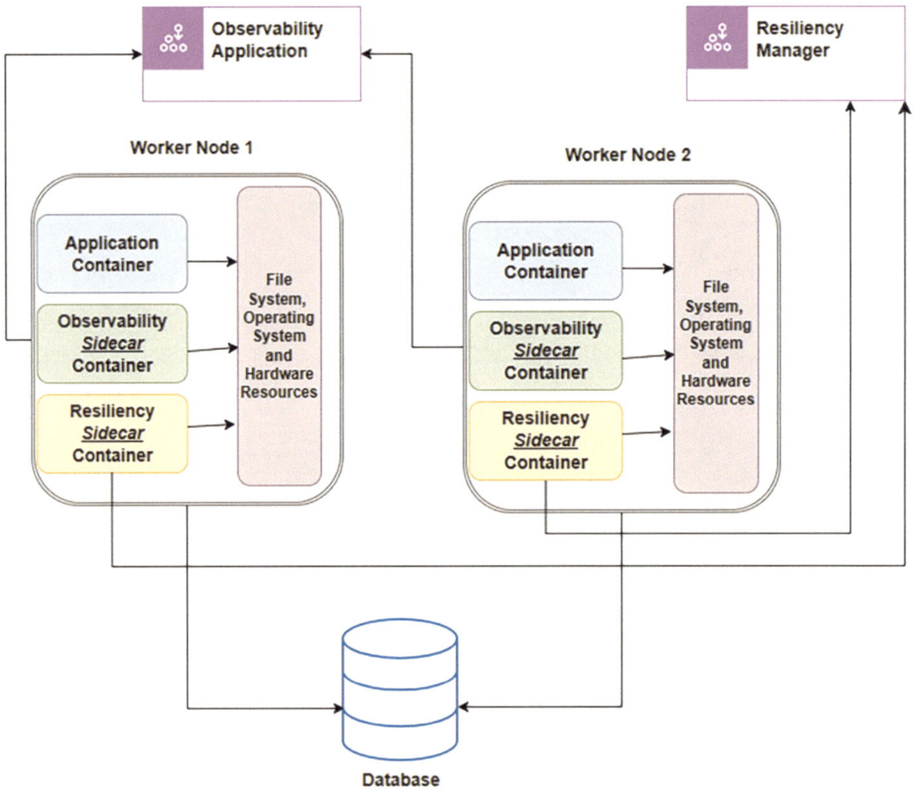


**Figure 5.**
*Sidecar systems architecture.*

When you are citing sources, the citations should be set in numbered format. All the references given in the list of references should be cited in the body of the text. Please set citations in square brackets keeping the below points in mind:

### 2.6 Trace ID and span ID

The Trace Id and Span id [8] are essential concepts in Distributed Systems from Observability point of view and they are used to track and monitor requests as they flow through a system, enabling easier troubleshooting and performance optimization.

A trace ID is a unique identifier that represents an end-to-end business process or request as it flows through a distributed system. It is used to group all the individual

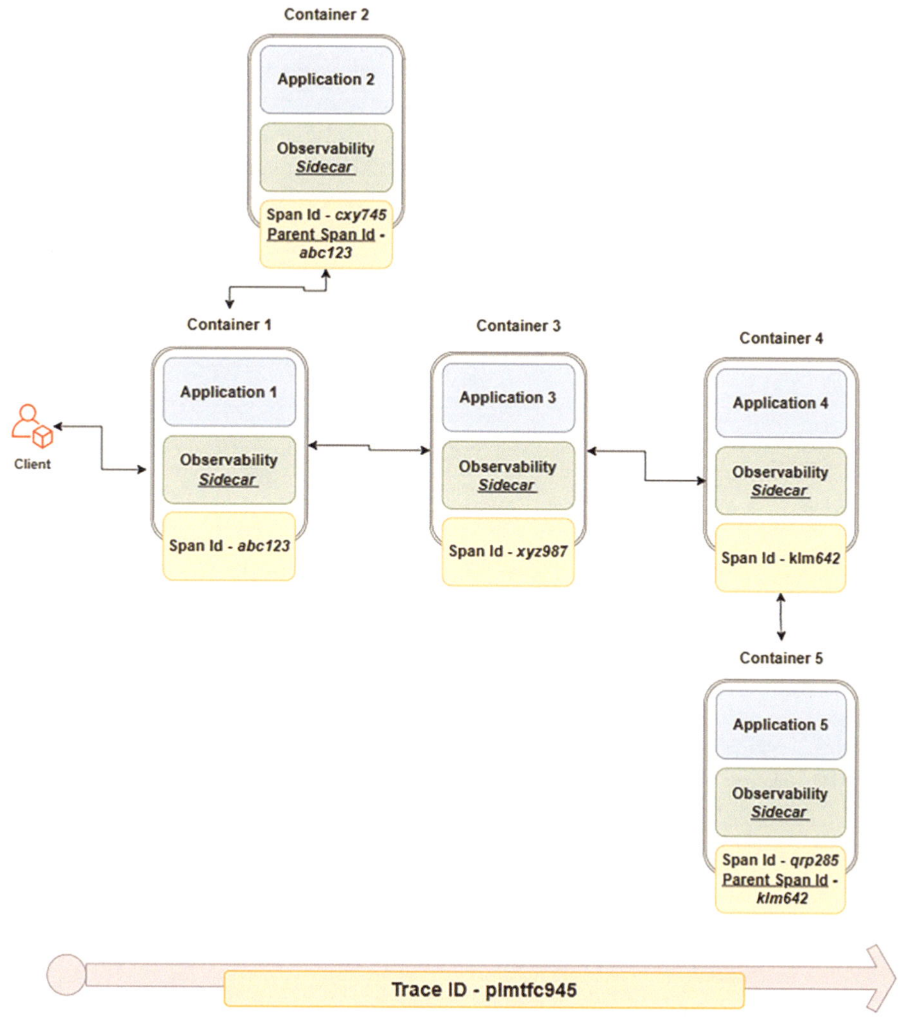


**Figure 6.**
*Trace Id and span Id capturing.*

spans that are part of a distributed transaction or request. A span ID, on the other hand, is a unique identifier for a single operation or unit of work within a distributed transaction or request. Spans are hierarchical and can be nested within a trace to represent the different components, services, or processes involved in handling a single request.

To implement tracing in a distributed system, applications need to instrument their code with a tracing sidecar, creating spans around operations they want to track. The tracing sidecar will then propagate the trace context from one service to another, allowing for the creation of a complete trace. Context propagation is the process of passing trace ID and span ID, as metadata along with each request to downstream services. This enables the reconstruction of the full execution of the request by grouping records based on the trace ID. The metadata also includes additional details such as tags and logs, which provide extra information for analysis and debugging (**Figure 6**).

## 2.7 Querying the trace and span

Traces can be queried using a columnar store, allowing applications to retrieve specific traces and analyze their performance. The query can be performed using a trace ID, which uniquely identifies the trace, and can be used to retrieve all spans associated with that trace. Traces can also be filtered using various parameters, such as service name, operation name, and duration. The results from the query allows applications to understand the flow of requests through their system and identify performance bottlenecks (**Tables 1** and **2**).

*SELECT trace_id WHERE trace_start_time > to_time('02-Jun-2025 10.02.23') and trace_end_time < to_time('02-Jun-2025 10.02.25');*

| trace_id |
|---|
| plmtfc945 |
| vrxewz034 |
| mcerop749 |

**Table 1.**
*Trace.*

*SELECT trace_id, app_name, span_id, parent_span_id, trace_start_time, trace_end_time, span_start_time, span_end_time WHERE trace_id =* ***"plmtfc945"****;*

| trace_id | app_name | span_id | trace_start_time | span_start_time | span_end_time | trace_end_time |
|---|---|---|---|---|---|---|
| plmtfc945 | Application 1 | abc123 | 02-Jun-2025 10.02.23.765 | 02-Jun-2025 10.02.24.342 | 02-Jun-2025 10.02.24.647 | |
| plmtfc945 | Application 2 | cxy745 | 02-Jun-2025 10.02.23.765 | 02-Jun-2025 10.02.24.473 | 02-Jun-2025 10.02.24.526 | |
| plmtfc945 | Application 3 | xyz987 | 02-Jun-2025 10.02.23.765 | 02-Jun-2025 10.02.24.648 | 02-Jun-2025 10.02.24.812 | |
| plmtfc945 | Application 4 | klm642 | 02-Jun-2025 10.02.23.765 | 02-Jun-2025 10.02.24.813 | 02-Jun-2025 10.02.24.956 | 02-Jun-2025 10.02.24.958 |
| plmtfc945 | Application 5 | qrp285 | 02-Jun-2025 10.02.23.765 | 02-Jun-2025 10.02.24.861 | 02-Jun-2025 10.02.24.914 | |

**Table 2.**
*Trace context.*

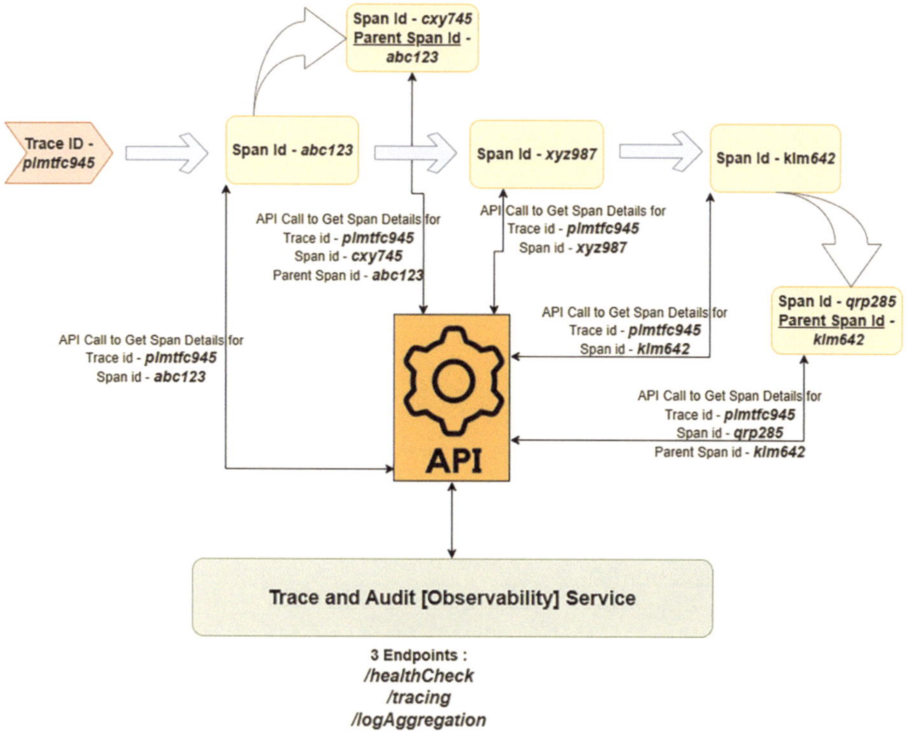


**Figure 7.**
*Visualizing the flow traces.*

## 2.8 Visualizing the trace and spans

By building a user interface by including searching and visualizing the flow of traces will provide valuable insights into system details. By analyzing traces, developers can identify bottlenecks and areas for optimization, leading to improved system performance and reliability (**Figure** 7).

## 2.9 Sample trace and span for distributed tracing

```
{
 "trace_context":{.
   "trace_id":"DT_kDMI7LTxLxTj220awNARJw==",
   "trace_start_time":"2025-2105-24 13:06:01.209458162 + 0000 UTC",
   "trace_end_time":"2025-2105-24 13:06:02.339515678 + 0000 UTC",
   "trace_attributes":
[
     {
       "key":"client.request.ip",
       "value":{.
       "stringValue":"212.10.0.45".
       }
     },
```

{
  "key":"auth.key",
  "value":{.
  "stringValue":"##5765FDET".
  }
},
{
  "key":"**observability.scope**",
  "value":{.
  "stringValue":"**Distributed_Tracing**".
  }
}
]
},
"resource_details":{.
 "app_name":"application1",
 "component":"/v1/application1/endpoint1",
 "region":"EAST",
 "data_center_location":"".
},
"span_details":{.
 "sub_component_name":"façade_layer",
 "span_id":"9ir6veJ4Hdw = ",
 "parent_span_id":"anir6veJ4Hdw = ",
 "span_start_time":"2025-2105-24 13:06:01.2351634953 + 0000 UTC",
 "span_end_time":"2025-2105-24 13:06:01.2421634271 + 0000 UTC",
 "status_code":"STATUS_CODE_OK",
 "status_message":"",
 "span_attributes":[.
  {
   "key":"task_status",
   "stringValue":"Success".
  },
  {
   "key":"time_taken",
   "intValue":312.
  }
 ]
}
}


## 2.10 Sample trace and span for health check


{
 "trace_context":{.
  "trace_id":"**HC**_rTSI7LTxLxTj220awNARJw–",
  "trace_start_time":"2025-2105-24 11:23:54.4569458592 + 0000 UTC",
  "trace_end_time":"2025-2105-24 11:23:54.9317814563 + 0000 UTC",
  "trace_attributes":[.
   {

```
        "key":"trace.type",
        "value":{.
         "stringValue":"cpu_utilization".
        }
      },
      {
        "key":"observability.scope",
        "value":{.
          "stringValue":"Health_Check".
        }
      }
    ]
  },
  "resource_details":{.
   "app_name":"application1",
   "component":"scanner",
   "region":"EAST",
   "data_center_location":"".
  },
  "span_details":{.
   "sub_component_name":"anti_virus",
   "span_id":"9ir6veJ4Hdw = ",
   "parent_span_id":"anir6veJ4Hdw = ",
   "span_start_time":"2025-2105-24 11:23:54.6849453821 + 0000 UTC",
   "span_end_time":"2025-2105-24 11:23:54.7046553129 + 0000 UTC",
   "span_attributes":[.
     {
       "key":"task_status",
       "stringValue":"Success".
     },
     {
       "key":"number_of_files_scanned",
       "intValue": 948667.
     }
   ]
  }
}
```

## 3. Conclusion

Observability-driven development is based on the principle of making systems more observable, which means being able to understand the internal state of a system by analyzing its external outputs. This approach encourages developers to implement observability from the start, rather than as an afterthought, by integrating logging, metrics, and tracing into their code. By analyzing and interpreting the data collected from observability tools to gain insights and perform needed actions. This can include identifying patterns and anomalies in the data, detecting performance bottlenecks, and optimizing system efficiency. It helps teams to understand internal system states without making arbitrary guesses, and to identify and address issues impacting system reliability and operational efficiency. Observability also enables teams to answer previously unknowable questions, and to address unknown unknowns, which is critical for complex distributed systems. For example, observability tools can help teams to debug application issues in a data-driven and repeatable manner, which can lead to cost savings from faster incident response and avoided incidents. It also enables organizations to identify areas for improvement, capture metrics, such as CPU usage and memory consumption, and provide alerts and notifications, and make informed decisions about resource allocation. Additionally, analytics on Observability data can help organizations detect security threats and respond to incidents more effectively. It is also essential to engage stakeholders from different business units and departments in discussions about observability's role in achieving organizational objectives and key results (OKRs).

## Author details

Rajasrikar Punugoti[1*] and Sirisha Manam[2]

1 Wells Fargo Bank, Cranbury, New Jersey, USA

2 Broadridge Financials, Fort Mill, South Carolina, USA

*Address all correspondence to: rajasrikarrao@gmail.com

## References

[1] singh P. Real-time insights in distributed systems: Advanced observability techniques for cloud-native enterprise architectures. International Journal of Core Engineering and Management [Internet]. 2023;(7):7. [cited 2025 Jun 13] Available from: https://ijcem.in/wp-content/uploads/2024/08/real-time-insights-in-distributed-systems.pdf

[2] opentelemetry Documentation. n.d. Available from: https://opentelemetry.io/docs/

[3] Koley S, Majumdar J, Bera MB, Acharjya PP. Multi-tenancy architecture for augmented security in cloud computing. In: 2023 5th International Conference on Inventive Research in Computing Applications (ICIRCA) - Multi-Tenancy Architecture for Augmented Security in Cloud Computing. Coimbatore, India: IEEE Conference Publication|IEEE Xplore; 2023

[4] Peterson CS. Investigating the Effect of Polyglot Programming on Developers. 10 Oct 2021:1-2. [cited 2024 Nov 5] Available from: https://ieeexplore.ieee.org/document/9576404

[5] Usman M, Ferlin S, Brunstrom A, Taheri J. A Survey on Observability of Distributed Edge and Container-Based Microservices. 2022. Available from: https://ieeexplore.ieee.org/document/9837035

[6] Cai L, Qi Y, Wei W, Li J. Improving Resource Usages of Containers through Auto-Tuning Container Resource Parameters - Improving Resource Usages of Containers through Auto-Tuning Container Resource Parameters. St Louis, MO, USA: IEEE Journals and Magazine|IEEE Xplore; 2019

[7] Salcedo-Navarro A, Garcia-Pineda M, Gutiérrez-Aguado J. K8sidecar: A Modular Kubernetes Chain of Sidecar Proxies for Microservices and Serverless Architectures - K8sidecar: A Modular Kubernetes Chain of Sidecar Proxies for Microservices and Serverless Architectures - Salcedo-Navarro - Software: Practice and Experience. St Louis, MO, USA: Wiley Online Library; 2025

[8] Jaeger Tracing Documentation. n.d. Available from: https://www.jaegertracing.io/docs/

Chapter 6

# Fast-Steered Minimum Variance Beamforming Algorithm

*Daizhu Zhu and Haoquan Guo*

## Abstract

The steered minimum variance (STMV) beamforming algorithm is highly regarded for its exceptional performance, characterized by high angular resolution, the absence of significant sidelobes, and excellent robustness. However, its practical application is severely limited by its computational demands. The core of the STMV algorithm is the inversion of an M $\times$ M covariance matrix, an operation with $O(M^3)$ complexity that must be repeated for every frequency bin and steering direction. This computational burden becomes prohibitive for large-scale arrays with many elements (M). Consequently, there is a critical need for simplified algorithms with lower complexity. This chapter introduces two novel algorithms: a block iterative steered minimum variance (BISTMV) beamformer and a regressive block iterative STMV (RBISTMV) beamformer. These methods dramatically reduce the computational workload to approximately 1/(4 M) of the conventional STMV algorithm for an M-element array. Through simulation analysis and processing of sea-trial data, we demonstrate that both proposed algorithms successfully retain the high angular resolution and multi-target detection capabilities of the original STMV. Their proven robustness paves the way for practical engineering implementation. Furthermore, the RBISTMV algorithm demonstrates an average improvement of $1 \sim 2$ dB in the directional index (DI) for moving targets compared to the standard STMV algorithm.

**Keywords:** beamforming, steered minimum variance (STMV), low complexity, block iterative, computational cost, multi-target detection, one-phase regressive filter

## 1. Introduction

High-resolution beamforming is a cornerstone technology for modern sonar, radar, and medical imaging systems. It provides the critical ability to detect, localize, and estimate parameters of targets, even when weak signals are obscured by strong, coherent interference. The steered minimum variance (STMV) beamforming algorithm is particularly prized for its ability to produce a narrow main beam, negligible sidelobes, and robust performance in challenging environments. Despite these advantages, its primary computational bottleneck—the inversion of an M $\times$ M covariance matrix for each steering angle and frequency, leading to an overall complexity of O ($M^3$)—renders conventional STMV impractical for real-time processing on arrays with hundreds of elements [1, 2].

 IntechOpen

This cubic scaling problem has motivated extensive research into four main strategies for complexity reduction:

1. Dimensionality reduction: These methods project the full-rank covariance matrix into a lower-dimensional subspace. Early examples include direct-separation adaptive beamforming, which reduces complexity with minimal performance loss [3], and steering-vector subspace methods that offer rapid convergence [4]. More recently, robust Capon beamforming within a Krylov subspace has been shown to cut multiplications by 15–20% and increase the output signal-to-interference-plus-noise ratio (SINR) by 3–5 dB when steering vectors are mismatched [5–7].

2. Recursive iteration: These techniques avoid full matrix inversions by using first-order updates or applying the matrix inversion lemma. The statistically optimized iterative MVDR algorithm achieves a per-update cost that is only 1/M of the classical STMV [8, 9], while a recursive MVDR approach further incorporates diagonal loading directly into the update steps [10].

3. Matrix decomposition: Instead of direct inversion, this approach uses methods like QR, Cholesky, or SVD decomposition, followed by efficient triangular system solves. Numerous hardware-friendly implementations and sub-array STMV frameworks based on these decompositions have been developed [11–18].

4. Matrix blocking: This strategy involves partitioning the large covariance matrix into smaller, more manageable sub-blocks. Methods based on Strassen's algorithm or block-Cholesky inversion can approach theoretical minimum FLOP counts, though they may suffer slight performance degradation by neglecting inter-block correlations [19–21].

Recent innovations continue to advance these paradigms. Liu et al. have shown that decomposing an aperture into single-sensor sub-arrays can eliminate matrix inversions entirely, capping the computational cost at $O(M^2)$ FLOPs while maintaining full-rank performance [22]. Wang et al. developed the IRDRCB method by embedding robust Capon beamforming in a Krylov subspace, reducing multiplications and boosting SINR under mismatch conditions [23]. Chen et al. proposed a method for coprime arrays that reconstructs the interference-plus-noise covariance on a virtual grid, achieving high accuracy with linear-time complexity [24]. For large-scale arrays, Zhang et al. reformulated sidelobe-constrained MVDR as a parallelizable ADMM problem with closed-form updates costing $O(M^2)$ per iteration [25]. In a departure from traditional signal processing, Goudarzi and Rivaz replaced all covariance operations with a deep learning U-Net, enabling kilohertz-rate imaging that matches MVDR-level quality [26].

Among these strategies, matrix decomposition offers significant arithmetic cost savings but often at the price of performance, as it approximates the solution by ignoring correlations between sub-blocks. Conversely, methods like those in Ref. [9] can achieve even lower complexity—reducing the inversion workload to just 2/M of the classical STMV—while preserving high-resolution performance.

To address the persistent challenge of cubic complexity, this paper introduces two novel algorithms: the block iterative STMV (BISTMV) [27, 28] and the regressive block iterative STMV (RBISTMV). Our approach employs a hierarchical, block-wise decomposition of the matrix inversion using the matrix inversion lemma. This strategy drastically reduces the overall computational burden, making high-performance beamforming viable for real-time systems. Simulation results and sea-trial data analysis confirm that our proposed algorithms match the performance of canonical STMV in resolution and interference suppression, but at a fraction of the computational cost.

## 2. Basic principles of STMV algorithm

The basic principle of STMV based on steered covariance matrix (STCM) is keeping the response at the steered bearing angle $\theta$ as 1 by rotating the beam and minimizing the total energy of output.

Assuming that each array output is $z(t) = [z_1(t), z_2(t), \cdots, z_M(t)]^T$.Correspondingly, frequency domain output is $Z(f_k)$.For conventional beam forming (CBF), according to the setting azimuth, each array output is inserted the time delay $\tau_m(\theta) = md\cos(\theta)/c, m = 0, \ldots, M-1$. The output after time delay is

$$Y(f_k, \theta) = \dot{T}_p(f_k, \theta)Z(f_k) \tag{1}$$

Where $M$ is the array number, $\theta$ is the bearing angle, $d$ is the interval between the adjacent array, $c$ is the acoustic speed, and $\dot{T}_p(f_k, \theta) = diag\left(\left[1, e^{j2\pi f_k d\cos(\theta)/c}, \cdots, e^{j2\pi f_k (M-1)d\cos(\theta)/c}\right]\right)$ is the steered matrix.

Assuming that the weight vector of each array is $w = [w_1, w_2, \cdots, w_M]^T$, the output of array is

$$y(t, \theta) = w^H \sum_{k=l}^{h} \dot{T}_p(f_k, \theta)Z(f_k)e^{j2\pi f_k t} \tag{2}$$

Where $h$ is the highest frequency point, and $l$ is the lowest one.

The average power of array output is

$$\begin{aligned} P(\theta) &= E\left[y(t,\theta)y(t,\theta)^H\right] \\ &= w^H E\left[\left(\sum_{k=l}^{h} \dot{T}_p(f_k,\theta)Z(f_k)\right)\left(\sum_{k=l}^{h} \dot{T}_p(f_k,\theta)Z(f_k)\right)^H\right] w \end{aligned} \tag{3}$$

Considering that $Z(f_k)$ and $Z(f_m)$ are uncorrelated when $T$ is large enough and $k \neq m$. Therefore

$$\begin{aligned} P(\theta) &= w^H E\left[\left(\sum_{k=l}^{h} \dot{T}_p(f_k,\theta)Z(f_k)\right)\left(\sum_{k=l}^{h} \dot{T}_p(f_k,\theta)Z(f_k)\right)^H\right] w \\ &= w^H E\left(\sum_{k=l}^{h}\sum_{m=l}^{h} \dot{T}_p(f_k,\theta)Z(f_k)Z^H(f_m)\dot{T}_p^H(f_m,\theta)\right) w \end{aligned} \tag{4}$$

$$
= w^H \left( \sum_{k=l}^{h} \dot{T}_P(f_k, \theta) E[Z(f_k) Z^H(f_k)] \dot{T}_p^H(f_k, \theta) \right) w
$$
$$
= w^H S_{stmv}(\theta) w
$$

Estimating the cross-spectral density matrix (CSDM) $S(f_k)$using the frequency domain output $Z_n(f_k)$ of $N$snapshots, shown as Eq. (5)

$$
S(f_k) = E[Z(f_k) Z^H(f_k)] = \sum_{n=1}^{N} Z_n(f_k) Z_n^H(f_k) \tag{5}
$$

Defining $S_{stmv}(\theta)$ as the STCM corresponding to the bearing angle $\theta$, shown as Eq. (6)

$$
S_{stmv}(\theta) = \sum_{k=l}^{h} \dot{T}_P(f_k, \theta) S(f_k) \dot{T}_p^H(f_k, \theta) \tag{6}
$$

The relationship between STCM and CSDM is also given by the formula.

The best weight vector of beam former is to keep the response as 1 at the specified direction, meanwhile minimize the power of array output, i.e.,

$$
\begin{cases} w = \arg[\min(w^H S_{stmv} w)] \\ w^H L_M = 1 \end{cases} \tag{7}
$$

Where $L_M$ is $M \times 1$vector of ones.

The weight vector can be obtained as Eq. (8) by applying the method of Lagrange multiplier.

$$
w = \frac{S_{stmv}^{-1}(\theta) L_M}{{L_M}^H S_{stmv}^{-1}(\theta) L_M} \tag{8}
$$

Substituting Eq. (8) into (4),

$$
P_{stmv}(\theta) = \frac{1}{{L_M}^H S_{stmv}^{-1}(\theta) L_M} \tag{9}
$$

STCM comprehensively utilizes information of each frequency, and the matrix is invertible if the product of frequency points and snapshots is bigger than order of the matrix.

## 3. The principle of fast-steered minimum variance

### 3.1 Principle of block matrix inverse

As for the inverse formula of $2 \times 2$ block matrix, it has been elaborated in Ref. [22]:

Lemma: Set $C = \begin{bmatrix} C_{11} & C_{12} \\ C_{12}^H & C_{22} \end{bmatrix}$, $C_{11}$and $C_{22}$ are $m$ order Hermitian matrix, and $C_{12}$ is $m$order matrix, then

$$C^{-1} = \begin{bmatrix} C_{11}^{-1} + C_{11}^{-1}C_{12}\left(C_{22} - C_{12}^H C_{11}^{-1} C_{12}\right)^{-1}\left(C_{11}^{-1}C_{12}\right)^H & -C_{11}^{-1}C_{12}\left(C_{22} - C_{12}^H C_{11}^{-1} C_{12}\right)^{-1} \\ \left(-C_{11}^{-1}C_{12}\left(C_{22} - C_{12}^H C_{11}^{-1} C_{12}\right)^{-1}\right)^H & \left(C_{22} - C_{12}^H C_{11}^{-1} C_{12}\right)^{-1} \end{bmatrix} \tag{10}$$

The inverse formula of $n \times n$ block matrix is derived as follow.

Theorem 1: Assume $C = \begin{bmatrix} C_{11} & C_{12} & C_{13} \\ C_{12}^H & C_{22} & C_{23} \\ C_{13}^H & C_{23}^H & C_{33} \end{bmatrix}$, $C_{11}$,$C_{22,}$ and $C_{33}$ are $m$ order Hermitian matrix, $C_{12}$, $C_{13,}$ and$C_{23}$ is $m$order matrix, then

$$C^{-1} = \begin{bmatrix} C_{11}^{-1} + DE^{-1}D^H & DE^{-1} \\ \left(DE^{-1}\right)^H & E^{-1} \end{bmatrix} \tag{11}$$

Where $D = \left(-C_{11}^{-1}C_{12}, \ -C_{11}^{-1}C_{13}\right)$, $E = \begin{bmatrix} C_{22} - C_{12}^H C_{11}^{-1} C_{12} & C_{23} - C_{12}^H C_{11}^{-1} C_{13} \\ \left(C_{23} - C_{12}^H C_{11}^{-1} C_{13}\right)^H & C_{33} - C_{13}^H C_{11}^{-1} C_{13} \end{bmatrix}$, the Eq. (11) is named as "combinational inverse formula".

Proof: Considering

$$\begin{aligned} &\begin{bmatrix} I_m & O_m & O_m \\ \left(-C_{11}^{-1}C_{12}\right)^H & I_m & O_m \\ \left(-C_{11}^{-1}C_{13}\right)^H & O_m & I_m \end{bmatrix} \begin{bmatrix} C_{11} & C_{12} & C_{13} \\ C_{12}^H & C_{22} & C_{23} \\ C_{13}^H & C_{23}^H & C_{33} \end{bmatrix} \begin{bmatrix} I_m & -C_{11}^{-1}C_{12} & -C_{11}^{-1}C_{13} \\ O_m & I_m & O_m \\ O_m & O_m & I_m \end{bmatrix} \\ &= \begin{bmatrix} C_{11} & O_m & O_m \\ O_m & C_{22} - C_{12}^H C_{11}^{-1} C_{12} & C_{23} - C_{12}^H C_{11}^{-1} C_{13} \\ O_m & \left(C_{23} - C_{12}^H C_{11}^{-1} C_{13}\right)^H & C_{33} - C_{13}^H C_{11}^{-1} C_{13} \end{bmatrix} \\ &= \begin{bmatrix} C_{11} & O_{m\times 2m} \\ O_{m\times 2m} & E \end{bmatrix} \end{aligned}$$

Then

$$\begin{aligned} C^{-1} &= \begin{bmatrix} I_m & D \\ O_{2m\times m} & I_{2m} \end{bmatrix} \begin{bmatrix} C_{11} & O_{m\times 2m} \\ O_{2m\times m} & E \end{bmatrix}^{-1} \begin{bmatrix} I_m & O_{m\times 2m} \\ D^H & I_{2m} \end{bmatrix} \\ &= \begin{bmatrix} I_m & D \\ O_{2m\times m} & I_{2m} \end{bmatrix} \begin{bmatrix} C_{11}^{-1} & O_{m\times 2m} \\ O_{2m\times m} & E^{-1} \end{bmatrix} \begin{bmatrix} I_m & O_{m\times 2m} \\ D^H & I_{2m} \end{bmatrix} \\ &= \begin{bmatrix} C_{11}^{-1} + DE^{-1}D^H & DE^{-1} \\ \left(DE^{-1}\right)^H & E^{-1} \end{bmatrix} \end{aligned}$$

Where, $E^{-1}$ can be derived by Eq. (10).

Theorem 2: Assuming that $C = \begin{bmatrix} C_{11} & C_{12} & C_{13} & C_{14} \\ C_{12}^H & C_{22} & C_{23} & C_{24} \\ C_{13}^H & C_{23}^H & C_{33} & C_{34} \\ C_{14}^H & C_{24}^H & C_{34}^H & C_{44} \end{bmatrix}$, $C_{11}$, $C_{22}$, $C_{33}$, and $C_{44}$ are $m$order Hermitian matrices, $C_{12}$, $C_{13}$, $C_{14}$, $C_{23}$, $C_{24}$, and $C_{34}$ are $m$order matrix, then

$$C^{-1} = \begin{bmatrix} C_{11}^{-1} + DE^{-1}D^H & DE^{-1} \\ (DE^{-1})^H & E^{-1} \end{bmatrix} \tag{12}$$

Where

$$D = \left(-C_{11}^{-1}C_{12},\ -C_{11}^{-1}C_{13},\ -C_{11}^{-1}C_{14}\right),$$

$$E = \begin{bmatrix} C_{22} - C_{12}^H C_{11}^{-1} C_{12} & C_{23} - C_{12}^H C_{11}^{-1} C_{13} & C_{24} - C_{12}^H C_{11}^{-1} C_{14} \\ \left(C_{23} - C_{12}^H C_{11}^{-1} C_{13}\right)^H & C_{33} - C_{13}^H C_{11}^{-1} C_{13} & C_{34} - C_{13}^H C_{11}^{-1} C_{14} \\ \left(C_{24} - C_{12}^H C_{11}^{-1} C_{14}\right)^H & \left(C_{34} - C_{13}^H C_{11}^{-1} C_{14}\right)^H & C_{44} - C_{14}^H C_{11}^{-1} C_{14} \end{bmatrix}$$

Illustration: It is not difficult to find out that in order to derive the inverse formula for the block matrix $C$ of $n \times n$ order, we can first solve $C_{11}^{-1}$, and then construct the matrices $D$ and $E$. Notice that $E$ is the block matrix of $(n-1) \times (n-1)$ order, we can apply the inverse formula $(n-1) \times (n-1)$ block matrix to solve $E^{-1}$. And so on, $C^{-1}$ can be derived with "combinational inverse formula", finally. This process is the basis for deriving the block matrix inverse calculation.

### 3.2 Principles of BISTMV algorithm

In STMV beamforming, the frequency domain output $Z_n(f_k)$ of $N$clips is summed, and the average frequency domain output is

$$\overline{Z}(f_k) = \sum_{n=1}^{N} Z_n(f_k) \tag{13}$$

Then the steered covariance matrix $S_{stmv}(\theta)$ can be expressed as

$$S_{stmv}(\theta) = \sum_{k=l}^{h} \dot{T}_p(f_k,\theta)\overline{Z}(f_k)\overline{Z}^H(f_k)\dot{T}_p^H(f_k,\theta) \tag{14}$$

Define $V = \dot{T}_p(f_k,\theta)\overline{Z}(f_k)$, then the Eq. (14) can be expressed as

$$S_{stmv}(\theta) = \sum_{k=l}^{h} VV^H \tag{15}$$

Assuming that $V$ is divided equally into $K$ segments, denoted as $V_i$,$i = 1, \cdots, K$, the length of each service is $k = M/K$. Then the steered covariance matrix $S_{stmv}(\theta)$ is divided equally into $K \times K$ blocks, and the order of each matrix is $k$. Considering that $S_{stmv}(\theta)$ is Hermitian matrix, the Eq. (15) can be expressed as.

$$S_{stmv}(\theta) = \begin{bmatrix} \sum_{i=l}^{h} V_1 V_1^H & \cdots & \sum_{i=l}^{h} V_1 V_K^H \\ \vdots & \ddots & \vdots \\ \left(\sum_{i=l}^{h} V_1 V_K^H\right)^H & \cdots & \sum_{i=l}^{h} V_K V_K^H \end{bmatrix} = \begin{bmatrix} S_{stmv}^{11}(\theta) & \cdots & S_{stmv}^{1K}(\theta) \\ \vdots & \ddots & \vdots \\ \left(S_{stmv}^{1K}(\theta)\right)^H & \cdots & S_{stmv}^{KK}(\theta) \end{bmatrix} \quad (16)$$

Apply the block matrix inverse formula to solve $S_{stmv}^{-1}(\theta)$, the algorithm idea and steps are as follows [23, 27, 28]:

1. First, solve $\left(S_{stmv}^{11}(\theta)\right)^{-1}$,

2. Constructing the matrix,

$$D = \left(-\left(S_{stmv}^{11}(\theta)\right)^{-1} S_{stmv}^{12}(\theta), \cdots, -\left(S_{stmv}^{11}(\theta)\right)^{-1} S_{stmv}^{1K}(\theta)\right) \quad (17)$$

$$E = \begin{bmatrix} S_{stmv}^{22}(\theta) - \left(S_{stmv}^{12}(\theta)\right)^H \left(S_{stmv}^{11}(\theta)\right)^{-1} S_{stmv}^{12}(\theta) & \cdots & S_{stmv}^{2K}(\theta) - \left(S_{stmv}^{12}(\theta)\right)^H \left(S_{stmv}^{11}(\theta)\right)^{-1} S_{stmv}^{1K}(\theta) \\ \vdots & \ddots & \vdots \\ \left(S_{stmv}^{2K}(\theta) - \left(S_{stmv}^{12}(\theta)\right)^H \left(S_{stmv}^{11}(\theta)\right)^{-1} S_{stmv}^{1K}(\theta)\right)^H & \cdots & S_{stmv}^{KK}(\theta) - \left(S_{stmv}^{1K}(\theta)\right)^H \left(S_{stmv}^{11}(\theta)\right)^{-1} S_{stmv}^{1K}(\theta) \end{bmatrix} \quad (18)$$

3. Apply block matrix inverse formula to recursively solve $E^{-1}$,

4. Apply "combination inverse formula" to solve $S_{stmv}^{-1}(\theta)$.

### 3.3 Principles of RBISTMV algorithm

In this algorithm, the former data are utilized sufficiently, one-phase regressive filter is used to integrate the covariance matrix $S_{stmv}(\theta)$, and then, STCM $\hat{S}_{stmv}(n)$ estimated by using the nth snapshot can be represented as [24]·

$$\hat{S}_{stmv}(n) = \alpha \hat{S}_{stmv}(n-1) + (1-\alpha) \sum_{k=l}^{h} V V^H \quad (19)$$

By matrix inversion lemma,

$$\left(C + xy^H\right)^{-1} = C^{-1} - \frac{C^{-1} x y^H C^{-1}}{1 + y^H C^{-1} x} \quad (20)$$

Therefore, $\hat{S}_{stmv}^{-1}(n)$ can be represented as

$$\begin{aligned}
\hat{S}^{-1}_{stmv}(n) &= \left[\alpha\hat{S}_{stmv}(n-1) + (1-\alpha)\sum_{k=l}^{h} VV^H\right]^{-1} \\
&= \left[\alpha\hat{S}_{stmv}(n-1) + (1-\alpha)\sum_{k=l}^{h-1} VV^H + (1-\alpha)V(f_h)V(f_h)^H\right]^{-1} \\
&= \tilde{S}^{-1}_{stmv}(h-1) - \frac{(1-\alpha)\tilde{S}^{-1}{}_{stmv}(h-1)V(f_h)V(f_h)^H\tilde{S}^{-1}{}_{stmv}(h-1)}{1+(1-\alpha)V(f_h)^H\tilde{S}^{-1}{}_{stmv}(h-1)V(f_h)}
\end{aligned} \tag{21}$$

Where $\tilde{S}_{stmv}(h-1) = \alpha\hat{S}_{stmv}(n-1) + (1-\alpha)\sum_{k=l}^{h-1} VV^H$. Obviously, in order to solve$\hat{S}^{-1}_{stmv}(n)$, we should solve $\tilde{S}^{-1}{}_{stmv}(h-1)$ first. Noting that $\tilde{S}_{stmv}(h-1)$ and $\hat{S}_{stmv}(n)$have the same form, and hence in order to solve$\tilde{S}^{-1}{}_{stmv}(h-1)$, we should solve $\tilde{S}^{-1}{}_{stmv}(h-2)$ first. By analogy, we can solve $\hat{S}^{-1}_{stmv}(n)$by iterative as long as $\tilde{S}^{-1}{}_{stmv}(l)$ is solved. $\tilde{S}^{-1}{}_{stmv}(l)$ can be represented as

$$\tilde{S}^{-1}{}_{stmv}(l) = \left[\alpha\hat{S}_{stmv}(n-1) + (1-\alpha)V(f_l)V^{\mathrm{H}}(f_l)\right]^{-1}$$

$$= \frac{1}{\alpha}\left[\hat{S}^{-1}{}_{stmv}(n-1) - \frac{(1-\alpha)\hat{S}^{-1}{}_{stmv}(n-1)V(f_l)V^{\mathrm{H}}(f_l)\hat{S}^{-1}{}_{stmv}(n-1)}{\alpha+(1-\alpha)V^{\mathrm{H}}(f_l)\hat{S}^{-1}{}_{stmv}(n-1)V(f_l)}\right] \tag{22}$$

Utilizing Eqs. (21) and (22) comprehensively, $\hat{S}^{-1}_{stmv}(n)$ can be estimated by $h-l$ iterations.

Then Eq. (15) can be represented as

$$S_{stmv}(\theta) = \begin{bmatrix}
\sum_{i=l}^{h} V_1V_1^H & \sum_{i=l}^{h} V_1V_2^H & \cdots & \sum_{i=l}^{h} V_1V_K^H \\
\left(\sum_{i=l}^{h} V_1V_2^H\right)^H & \sum_{i=l}^{h} V_2V_2^H & \cdots & \sum_{i=l}^{h} V_2V_K^H \\
\vdots & \vdots & \ddots & \vdots \\
\left(\sum_{i=l}^{h} V_1V_K^H\right)^H & \left(\sum_{i=l}^{h} V_2V_K^H\right)^H & \cdots & \sum_{i=l}^{h} V_KV_K^H
\end{bmatrix} \tag{23}$$

Assuming that STCM $\hat{S}_{stmv}(n)$ estimated by using the nth snapshot is segmented equally into $K \times K$parts, calling $\hat{S}^{ij}_{stmv}(n)$, where $i,j = 1, \ldots K$. Considering $\hat{S}_{stmv}(n)$ is Hermitian matrix, then Eq. (19) can be represented as.

$$\begin{bmatrix} \hat{S}^{11}_{stmv}(n) & \hat{S}^{12}_{stmv}(n) & \cdots & \hat{S}^{1K}_{stmv}(n) \\ \left(\hat{S}^{12}_{stmv}(n)\right)^H & \hat{S}^{22}_{stmv}(n) & \cdots & \hat{S}^{2K}_{stmv}(n) \\ \vdots & \vdots & \ddots & \vdots \\ \left(\hat{S}^{1K}_{stmv}(n)\right)^H & \left(\hat{S}^{2K}_{stmv}(n)\right)^H & \cdots & \hat{S}^{KK}_{stmv}(n) \end{bmatrix} = \alpha \begin{bmatrix} \hat{S}^{11}_{stmv}(n-1) & \hat{S}^{12}_{stmv}(n-1) & \cdots & \hat{S}^{1K}_{stmv}(n-1) \\ \left(\hat{S}^{12}_{stmv}(n-1)\right)^H & \hat{S}^{22}_{stmv}(n-1) & \cdots & \hat{S}^{2K}_{stmv}(n-1) \\ \vdots & \vdots & \ddots & \vdots \\ \left(\hat{S}^{1K}_{stmv}(n-1)\right)^H & \left(\hat{S}^{2K}_{stmv}(n-1)\right)^H & \cdots & \hat{S}^{KK}_{stmv}(n-1) \end{bmatrix}$$
$$+(1-\alpha)\begin{bmatrix} \sum_{i=l}^{h} V_1V_1^H & \sum_{i=l}^{h} V_1V_2^H & \cdots & \sum_{i=l}^{h} V_1V_K^H \\ \left(\sum_{i=l}^{h} V_1V_2^H\right)^H & \sum_{i=l}^{h} V_2V_2^H & \cdots & \sum_{i=l}^{h} V_2V_K^H \\ \vdots & \vdots & \ddots & \vdots \\ \left(\sum_{i=l}^{h} V_1V_K^H\right)^H & \left(\sum_{i=l}^{h} V_2V_K^H\right)^H & \cdots & \sum_{i=l}^{h} V_KV_K^H \end{bmatrix} \tag{24}$$

Applying inversion formula of block matrix equation to solving $\hat{S}^{-1}_{stmv}(n)$, the basic principle is

1. Solving $\left(\hat{S}^{11}_{stmv}(n)\right)^{-1}$ by iterative Eqs. (21) and (22);

2. Constructing matrices

$$D = \left(-\left(\hat{S}^{11}_{stmv}(n)\right)^{-1}\hat{S}^{12}_{stmv}(n), \ldots, -\left(\hat{S}^{11}_{stmv}(n)\right)^{-1}\hat{S}^{1K}_{stmv}(n)\right) \tag{25}$$

$$E = \begin{bmatrix} \hat{S}^{22}_{stmv}(n) - \left(\hat{S}^{12}_{stmv}(n)\right)^H\left(\hat{S}^{11}_{stmv}(n)\right)^{-1}\hat{S}^{12}_{stmv}(n) & \cdots & \hat{S}^{2K}_{stmv}(n) - \left(\hat{S}^{12}_{stmv}(n)\right)^H\left(\hat{S}^{11}_{stmv}(n)\right)^{-1}\hat{S}^{1K}_{stmv}(n) \\ \vdots & \ddots & \vdots \\ \left(\hat{S}^{2K}_{stmv}(n) - \left(\hat{S}^{12}_{stmv}(n)\right)^H\left(\hat{S}^{11}_{stmv}(n)\right)^{-1}\hat{S}^{1K}_{stmv}(n)\right)^H & \cdots & \hat{S}^{KK}_{stmv}(n) - \left(\hat{S}^{1K}_{stmv}(n)\right)^H\left(\hat{S}^{11}_{stmv}(n)\right)^{-1}\hat{S}^{1K}_{stmv}(n) \end{bmatrix} \tag{26}$$

3. Applying inversion formula of block matrix to solving $E^{-1}$ recursively;

4. Applying "combination inversion formula" to solving $\hat{S}^{-1}_{stmv}(\theta)$.

## 4. Analysis of calculation complexity

### 4.1 Complexity of classic STMV algorithm

Noting that computing cost of multiplication is tens of times of add operation, so this paper only takes computational cost of multiplication into consideration.

Assuming that array number is $M$, the bandwidth of signal is $B$, and CSDM is estimated by the frequency domain output of $N$snapshots. The computational cost of STMV is mainly focused on two parts as follows:

1. The CSDM is estimated with Eq. (5). It should be multiplied $M^2$ times at each frequency point, and $M^2NB$ times of multiplication operation is necessary in all;

2. The following calculation is necessary for each beam while estimating spatial spectrum:

   a. The STCM is estimated with Eq. (6). It should be multiplied $2M^2$ times at each frequency point, and $2M^2B$ times of multiplication operation is necessary in all;

   b. The inversion operation of STCM needs $M^3$ times of multiplication operation, and then, it should be multiplied $M^2 + M$ times while estimating spatial spectrum with Eq. (9).

In summary, assuming the beam number is $L$, then the total times of multiplication operation are

$$NM^2B + \left[M^3(2B+1) + M^2 + M\right]L \tag{27}$$

### 4.2 Complexity of BISTMV algorithm

Assuming that $G(m)$ is the calculation amount of inverse $m$–order matrix, then the calculation amount of inverse of $2 \times 2$ as Eq. (10) and $3 \times 3$ block matrix as Eq. (11) is, respectively:

$$x_2 = 2G(m) + 4m^3 \tag{28}$$

$$x_3 = x_2 + G(m) + 11m^3 \tag{29}$$

The proof is the same as above. Where $E^{-1}$ can be derived by Eq. (11). According to Eqs. (12) and (11), the inversion computational cost of $4 \times 4$block matrix is

$$x_4 = x_3 + G(m) + 21m^3 \tag{30}$$

In summary, we consider the general formula of inversion computational cost of $n \times n$ block matrix. Inversion computational cost of $n \times n$ block matrix is

$$x_n = x_{n-1} + G(m) + \frac{5}{2}(n-1)m^3 + \frac{3}{2}(n-1)^2m^3 \tag{31}$$

Combining Eqs. (28), (29), and (30), we can derive the general formula

$$x_n = nG(m) + \frac{1}{2}\left((n-1)^3 + 4(n-1)^2 + 3(n-1)\right)m^3 \tag{32}$$

The calculation is mainly concentrated in three parts:

1. Using $V = \dot{T}_p(f_k, \theta)\overline{Z}(f_k)$ to solve $V$, $M^2$ multiplication is needed at each frequency point, and $M^2B$ multiplication is needed in total time.

2. To construct the matrix $S_{stmv}(\theta)$, the requirement solution $S^{11}_{stmv}(\theta), \dots, S^{1K}_{stmv}(\theta)$, $S^{22}_{stmv}(\theta), \dots, S^{2K}_{stmv}(\theta)$, $S^{33}_{stmv}(\theta), \dots, S^{3K}_{stmv}(\theta), \dots, S^{KK}_{stmv}(\theta)$, a total of $\frac{K(K+1)}{2}k^2B$ multiplication should be performed.

3. Using block matrix inverse formula to solve $S^{-1}_{stmv}(\theta)$, $KG(k) + \frac{1}{2}\left((K-1)^3 + 4(K-1)^2 + 3(K-1)\right)k^3$ multiplication is needed, then the space spectrum is estimated with Eq. (9), and $M^2 + M$ multiplication is needed.

In summary, it is assumed that the space spectrum estimation of $L$ beam is carried out, and the calculation amount required is

$$\left(M^2B + \frac{K(K+1)}{2}k^2B + KG(k) + \frac{1}{2}\left((K-1)^3 + 4(K-1)^2 + 3(K-1)\right)k^3 + M^2 + M\right)L \tag{33}$$

Where $G(k)$ is the calculation amount of the inverse of the $k$-order matrix, $G(k) = k^3$. At the same time, considering that $k = M/K$, the Eq. (33) is simplified as

$$\left(\left(\frac{3}{2} + \frac{1}{2K}\right)M^2B + \left(\frac{1}{2} + \frac{1}{2K}\right)M^3 + M^2 + M\right)L \tag{34}$$

In fact, when $V = \dot{T}_p(f_k, \theta)\overline{Z}(f_k)$ is used to solve $V$, considering that $\dot{T}_p(f_k, \theta, )$ is a diagonal matrix, its calculation can be reduced to $MB$, and then, the amount of computation required is

$$\left(\left(\frac{1}{2} + \frac{1}{2K}\right)M^2B + MB + \left(\frac{1}{2} + \frac{1}{2K}\right)M^3 + M^2 + M\right)L \tag{35}$$

### 4.3 Complexity of RBISTMV algorithm

The computational cost of RBISTMV algorithm is mainly focused on five parts as follows:

1. It should be multiplied by $M^2$ times at each frequency point when utilizing $V = \dot{T}_p(f_k, \theta)\overline{Z}(f_k)$ to solve $V$. $M^2B$ times of multiplication operation is necessary in all;

2. Each iteration operation needs $3k^2 + k$ times of multiplication operation at each frequency point when solving $\left(\hat{S}^{11}_{stmv}(n)\right)^{-1}$ according to Eqs. (21) and (22). $(3k^2 + k)B$ times of multiplication operation is necessary in all;

3. In order to construct matrices $D$ and $E$, it needs to solve $\hat{S}^{12}_{stmv}(n), \dots, \hat{S}^{1K}_{stmv}(n)$, $\hat{S}^{22}_{stmv}(n), \dots, \hat{S}^{2K}_{stmv}(n)$, $\hat{S}^{33}_{stmv}(n), \dots, \hat{S}^{3K}_{stmv}(n), \dots, \hat{S}^{KK}_{stmv}(n)$. $\left(\frac{K(K+1)}{2} - 1\right)k^2B$ times of multiplication operation is necessary in all;

4. Applying inversion formula of block matrix to solving $E^{-1}$ recursively, it should be multiplied by $(K-1)G(k)+\frac{1}{2}\left((K-2)^3+4(K-2)^2+3(K-2)\right)k^3$ times;

5. 5.Applying "combination inversion formula" to solving$S_{stmv}^{-1}(\theta)$, it should be multiplied by $(K-1)^2k^3+(K-1)k^3$ times. Then it should be multiplied $M^2+M$ times while estimating spatial spectrum with Eq. (9).

In summary, assuming the beam number is $L$, then the total times of multiplication operation is

$$\left(M^2B+(3k^2+k)B+\left(\frac{K(K+1)}{2}-1\right)k^2B+(K-1)G(k)\right)L$$
$$+\left(\frac{1}{2}\left((K-2)^3+4(K-2)^2+3(K-2)\right)k^3+(K-1)^2k^3+(K-1)k^3+M^2+M\right)L \tag{36}$$

Where the computational cost of $k$order inverse matrix is $G(k)$, where $G(k)=k^3$. Considering $k=M/K$ meanwhile, Eq. (36) can be simplified to

$$\left(\left(\frac{3}{2}+\frac{1}{2K}+\frac{2}{K^2}\right)M^2B+\frac{1}{K}MB+\left(\frac{1}{2}-\frac{1}{2K^2}\right)M^3+M^2+M\right)L \tag{37}$$

Illustration: In fact, considering $\dot{T}_p(f_k,\theta)$is diagonal matrix, the computational cost can be reduced to $MB$ when utilizing $V=\dot{T}_p(f_k,\theta)\overline{Z}(f_k)$ to solve $V$. Now, the total times of multiplication operation

$$\left(\left(\frac{1}{2}+\frac{1}{2K}+\frac{2}{K^2}\right)M^2B+\left(1+\frac{1}{K}\right)MB+\left(\frac{1}{2}-\frac{1}{2K^2}\right)M^3+M^2+M\right)L \tag{38}$$

Assuming that the bandwidth of signal $B$ =5kHz and a beam is formed every$2^\circ$ in the range of $0^\circ \sim 180^\circ$; that is to say, it should estimate spatial spectrum at $L$ =91 beams. The snapshot is $N=4$, $K$ =20. Then, the ratio of computational cost between the STMV algorithm and BISTMV, RBISTMV algorithms for various array number $M$ is shown in **Figure 1**.

They are almost same ratio of calculation cost between the classical STMV algorithm and BISTMV, STMV and RBISTMV algorithm for various array number $M$in **Figure 1**, and it means that the difference of calculation cost between BISTMV and RBISTMV algorithms is negligible.

The computational cost of iterative algorithm proposed in Ref. [9] is approximately $2/M$times of computational cost of STMV algorithm. In order to facilitate analysis, if we take into account both $L \gg N$ and $B \gg M$, Eqs. (27), (35), (38) can be simplified, respectively, to $2M^3BL$, $\left(\frac{1}{2}+\frac{1}{2K}\right)(M^2B+M^3)L$and $\frac{(M^2B+M^3)L}{2}+\frac{M^2BL}{2K}$. Then the ratio of computational cost of two algorithms is

$$\frac{\left(\frac{1}{2}+\frac{1}{2K}\right)(M^2B+M^3)L}{2M^3BL}=\frac{\left(1+\frac{1}{K}\right)\left(1+\frac{M}{B}\right)}{4M}\approx\frac{1}{4M} \tag{39}$$

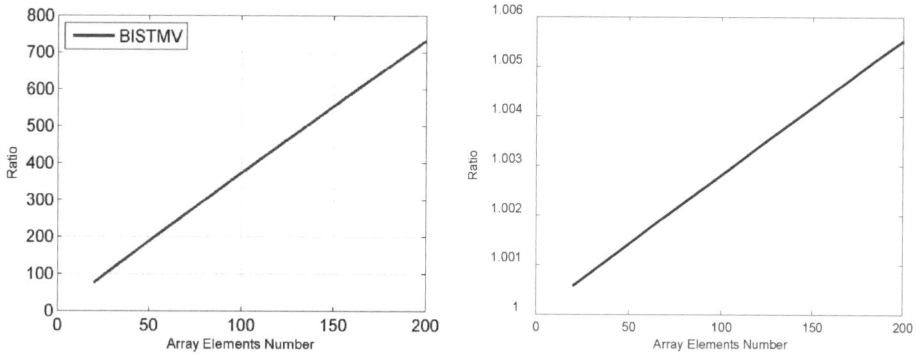


**Figure 1.**
*Ratio of calculation cost between the classical STMV algorithm and BISTMV, and the ratio of calculation cost between BISTMV and RBISTMV for various array number M.*

$$\frac{\frac{(M^2B+M^3)L}{2}+\frac{M^2BL}{2K}}{2M^3BL}=\frac{1+\frac{M}{B}+\frac{1}{K}}{4M}\approx\frac{1}{4M} \tag{40}$$

According to Eqs. (39) and (40), both computational cost of BISTMV and RBISTMV algorithms proposed in this chapter are close to $1/4M$ times of the computational cost of original algorithm. The computational cost drops dramatically when $M \gg 5$.

To demonstrate the real-world impact, a benchmark test was conducted on an AMD EPYC 7742 CPU using data from a 256-element array, forming 90 beams. The conventional STMV algorithm required 220 seconds to process a 2-second data segment, whereas our BISTMV algorithm finished the same task in only 0.271 seconds. This represents an 800-fold speedup, transforming the process from a slow, offline task to one capable of continuous, real-time operation.

## 5. Simulation and analysis

### 5.1 Azimuth resolution

The simulation conditions are listed as follows. Two sources' signals and background noise defined over the same frequency band 0.05 fs $\sim$ 0.25 fs are Gaussian white noise which are independent with each other. The signal-to-noise ratio (SNR) of each source is 0 dB, sampling frequency is fs, and sound speed is 1500 m/s. The receiver is a uniformly spaced linear array of 48 sensors with inter-element spacing of $d$, corresponding to the maximum frequency. The length of each snapshot is 0.8 s, and the integration time of beam former is 3.2 s, where $\alpha = 2/3$. The bearing angles of two sources are assumed in two conditions: 80°and 88°, 80°and 84°. The spatial spectrum estimated by STMV algorithm and BISTMV, RBISTMV algorithms ($K = 6$) are shown in **Figure 2**.

The simulation results in **Figure 2** show that both BISTMV and RBISTMV successfully resolve the two targets in both scenarios. Their spatial spectra are nearly identical to that of the classical STMV algorithm, demonstrating that the sharp reduction in computational cost does not sacrifice azimuth resolution or main-lobe width. RBISTMV shows a slightly higher peak, indicating an improvement in the directional index (DI) due to its use of a regressive filter.

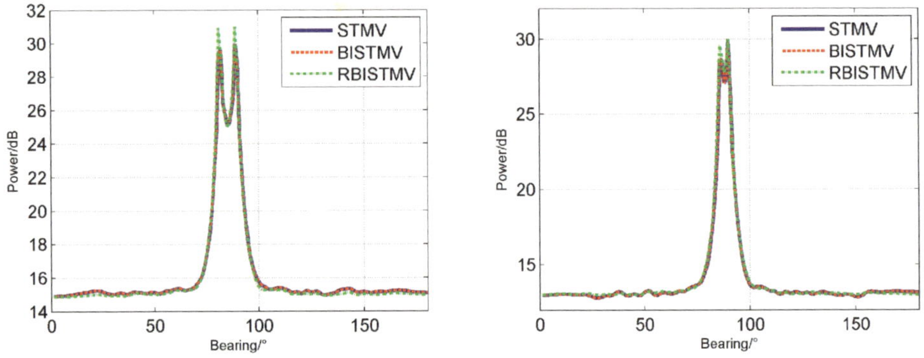


(a) Two sources lie at 80° and 88°

(b) Two sources lie at 80° and 84°

**Figure 2.**
*Comparison of STMV algorithm and BISTMV, RBISTMV algorithms on spatial spectrum.*

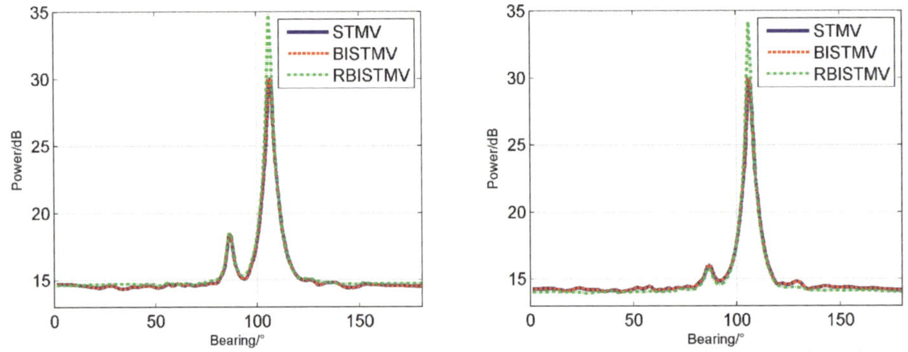


(a) SNR=5dB and -15dB

(b) SNR=5dB and -20dB

**Figure 3.**
*Comparison of three algorithms on spatial spectrum in different SNR.*

### 5.2 Ability of detecting weak source

The simulation conditions are listed as follows. There is an interference lied at the bearing angle 100° with SNR = 5 dB, and weak target source lied at the bearing angle 80°. The simulation is in two conditions: SNR = −15 dB and SNR = −20 dB, other parameters are the same as the former. The spatial spectrum estimated by STMV algorithm and BISTMV, RBISTMV algorithms are shown in **Figure 3**.

As shown in **Figure 3**, both BISTMV and RBISTMV inherit STMV's excellent ability to detect weak targets in the presence of strong interference. Even when the target is 25 dB weaker than the interferer, it is clearly detected by all three algorithms. This confirms that the proposed methods maintain the robustness required for detecting weak signals in complex environments, with RBISTMV again showing a slight DI advantage.

## 6. Analysis on sea-trial data

To validate the algorithms with real-world data, we analyzed data from a sea trial involving a 48-element uniform linear array towed by a vessel.

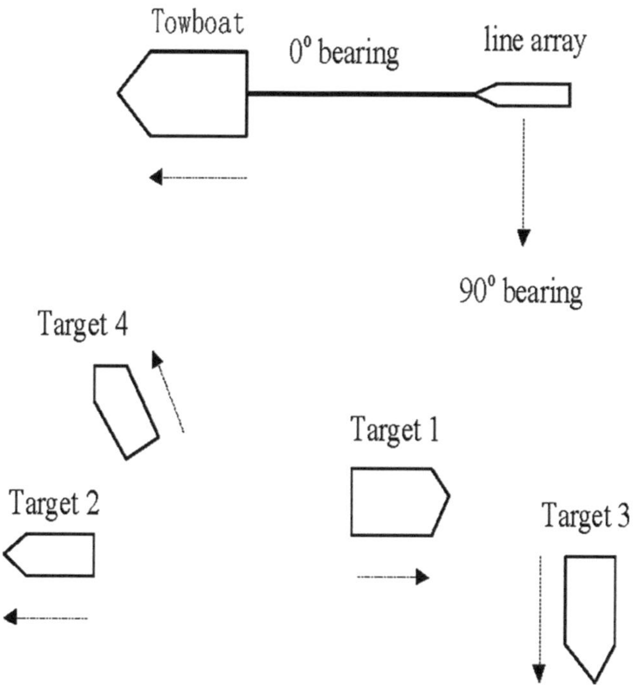


**Figure 4.**
*Trail frame.*

The towboat was on a straight course (0°). Target 2 started at an approximate bearing of 75° and moved parallel to the towboat. Target 4 moved toward the array. Targets 1 and 3 were strong contacts moving away from the towboat (**Figure 4**).

The course diagrams produced by STMV, BISTMV, and RBISTMV (**Figures 5–7**) are virtually indistinguishable, demonstrating the reliability of the fast algorithms.

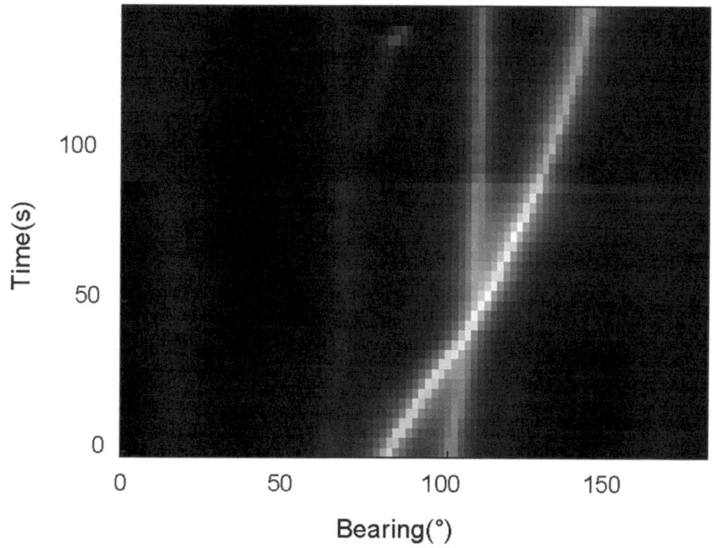


**Figure 5.**
*Diagram of STMV.*

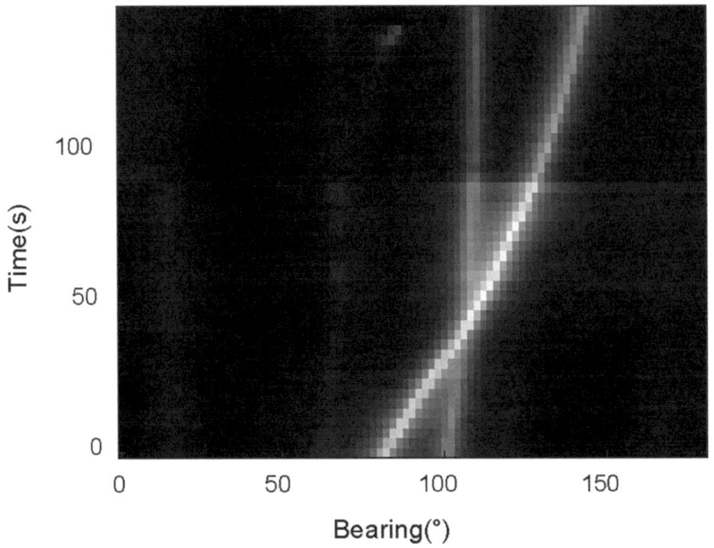


**Figure 6.**
*Diagram of BISTMV.*

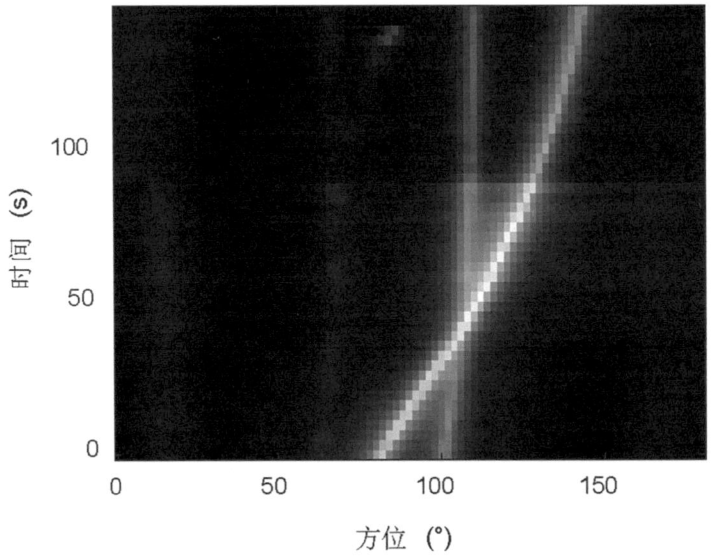


**Figure 7.**
*Diagram of RBISTMV.*

The RBISTMV diagram (**Figure 7**) clearly shows five targets, including the towboat's own noise at ~20°. The algorithms exhibit high resolution, for example, by discriminating Target 1 (~80°) and Target 3 (~100°) even as their bearings cross at the 40-second mark. Furthermore, two weak targets near 65° are successfully tracked as their bearings converge and then diverge.

To highlight the weak target detection performance, **Figures 8** and **9** show the spatial spectra at specific time points (68 s and 110 s).

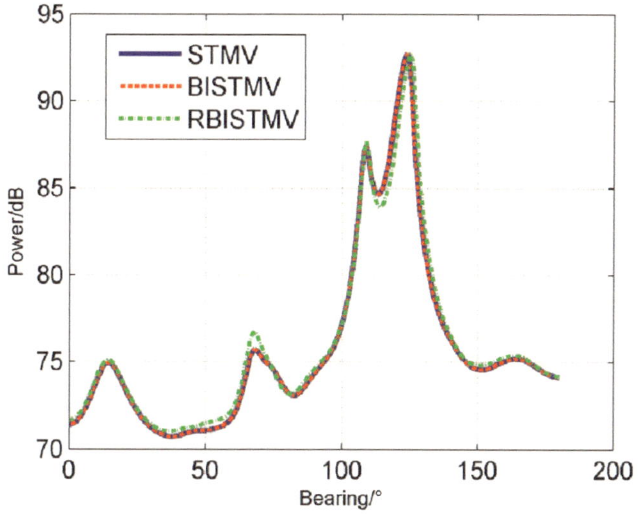


**Figure 8.**
*Spatial spectrum at 68 s.*

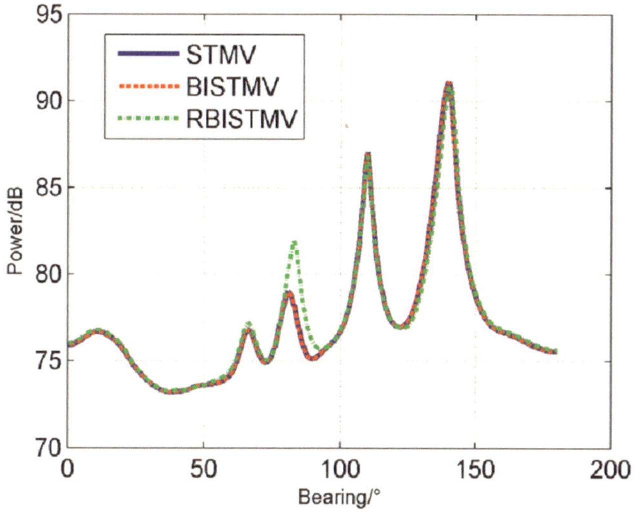


**Figure 9.**
*Spatial spectrum at 110 s.*

These snapshots confirm that even though Targets 2 and 4 have an SNR approximately 20 dB lower than Targets 1 and 3, they are still detected reliably by BISTMV and RBISTMV. The output of BISTMV is nearly identical to that of STMV. Crucially, for the moving Target 2, the RBISTMV algorithm achieves an average directional index improvement of $1 \sim 2$ dB over STMV. This gain is attributed to the one-phase regressive filter (Eq. 19), which effectively utilizes the temporal coherence of the target's signal as it moves, leading to superior estimation and enhanced performance.

## 7. Summary and discussion

This chapter first analyzed the prohibitive computational cost of the classical STMV algorithm, which restricts its use in practical, real-time engineering systems. To overcome this limitation, we proposed two novel fast algorithms: the BISTMV algorithm, based on block matrix inversion, and the RBISTMV algorithm, which further integrates a one-phase regressive filter.

The key findings are as follows:

1. Computational Efficiency: Both proposed algorithms reduce the computational load to approximately 1/(4 M) that of the classical STMV algorithm, making real-time application on large arrays feasible.

2. Performance Preservation: Simulation and sea-trial data processing confirmed that BISTMV and RBISTMV retain the signature advantages of STMV, including high azimuth resolution and robust multi-target detection. They can effectively detect weak targets even in the presence of strong interference and closely-spaced signals.

3. Performance Enhancement: The RBISTMV algorithm demonstrated a performance improvement, achieving a $1 \sim 2$ dB higher directional index for moving targets by exploiting signal coherence over time via its regressive filter.

These advancements establish a solid foundation for the engineering application of STMV, enabling high-performance, high-resolution beamforming in real-time systems where it was previously computationally impossible.

## Author details

Daizhu Zhu* and Haoquan Guo
Shanghai Marine Electronic Equipment Research Institute, Shanghai, China

*Address all correspondence to: zdz91511@sina.com

## References

[1] Van Tree L. Optimum Array Processing. New York: John Wiley and Sons Inc.; 2003. p. 48

[2] Yongliang W. Theory and Algorithm on Spatial Spectrum Estimation. Beijing: Tsinghua University Press; 2004 (in Chinese)

[3] Yuning Q, Xinrong C, Yawei C, et. The blind separation for passive sonar-research on adaptive beamforming. Journal of electric and information. 2017; **39**(10):2390-2396 (in Chinese)

[4] Jianping X, Rui W, et. The research on optimal adaptive beamforming with steered vector and combining iteration. Journal of Acoustic. 2016;**41**(3):343-352 (in Chinese)

[5] Samuel Somasundaram, et al. Data-Adaptive Reduced-Dimension Robust Capon Beamforming, Acoustics, Speech and Signal Processing (ICASSP). 2013

[6] Somasundaram S et al. Reduced-dimension robust capon beamforming using Krylov-subspace techniques. IEEE Transactions on Aerospace and Electronic Systems. 2015;**51**(1):270-289

[7] Liankun B, Zhang xiaoyong, Xiong Jingyu. The robust capon beamforming on distorted towed line array. Journal of Electric and Information. 2018;**40**(10): 142-148

[8] Pados DA, Karystinos GN. An iterative algorithm for the computation of the MVDR filter. IEEE Transactions on Signal Processing. 2001;**49**(2): 290-300

[9] Daizhu Z, Guangfang L, Junying H, et al. Iterative algorithm of steered minimum variance and its application in weak targets detection. Journal of Shanghai Jiaotong University (Science). 2010;**15**:56-63

[10] Chen MS, Liou RJ. Recursive MVDR for direction finding using circular arrays. In: International Symposium on Antenna Technology and Applied Electromagnetics and Ursi Conference. IEEE; 2017

[11] Zeng Zhaohua, Zhang Jianhong, Zhao Qian. Research of Adaptive Beamforming Algorithm Based on Matrix Decomposition. 2010 (in Chinese)

[12] Rabinkin DV. Adaptive array beamforming with fixed-point arithmetic matrix inversion using givens rotations. Proceedings of SPIE - The International Society for Optical Engineering. 2001;**4474**:294-305

[13] Mohan CS, Menon SB, Nissar KE, et al. Adaptive beamforming with instantaneous convergence and its efficient implementation in DSP hardware. India Conference. IEEE. 2013

[14] Wang SS, Tien YC, Hwang YT, et al. MVDR Based Adaptive Beamformer Design and its FPGA Implementation for Ultrasonic Imaging. IEEE: Circuits and Systems; 2016

[15] Yijun Z, Qianli L. The parallel realization of STMV beamforming algorithm. Computer and Digit Engineering. 2017;**45**(9):1731-1735 (in Chinese)

[16] Swingler D. A low-complexity MVDR beamformer for use with short observation times. Proceeding of the IEEE. 1999;**47**(4):1154-1160

[17] Zhou Shengzeng DU, Xuanmin. Research and application of fast-

convergent minimum variance distortionless response algorithm. Chinese Journal of Acoustics. 2009;**34**: 515-520 (in Chinese)

[18] Bin QIAN, Ping WANG, Xin WANG. Subarray optimization and partition technology in dimension reduction steered minimum variance. Journal of Harbin Engineering University. 2013;**34**:445-449 (in Chinese)

[19] Fei G, Yongliang W, et. Research on inversion matrix of STAP. The Science and Technology on Radar. 2008;**6**(3): 215-218 (in Chinese)

[20] Rui L, Xiaoming L, Ye D. The fast algorithm on STAP matrix. Computer Simulation. 2011;**28**(2) (in Chinese)

[21] Tinghui C, Jianping C. The New Method on Inverse Covariance Matrix of STAP. The 16th Conference on Information of Chinese Electronic Association (Part 3: Signal Processing) 2019. pp. 479-483 (in Chinese)

[22] Liu T et al. Reduced-dimension MVDR beamformer based on sub-array optimisation. IET Communications. 2022;**16**(2):165-173

[23] Wang X, Jiang X, Chen Y. Improved reduced-dimension robust capon beamforming using Krylov subspace techniques. Sensors. 2024;**24**(22):7152

[24] Chen S et al. Efficient and robust adaptive beamforming based on coprime array interpolation. Remote Sensing. 2024;**16**(15):2792

[25] Zhang W et al. A distributed approach to robust MVDR beamforming in large-scale arrays. IET Communications. 2023;**17**(8):950-959

[26] Goudarzi S, Rivaz H. Plane-wave ultrasound beamforming: A deep learning approach. Ultrasonics. 2021;**118**: 106780

[27] Daizhu Z, Haoquan G, et al. Block iterative STMV algorithm and its application in multi-targets detection. Journal of Applied Mathematics and Physics. 2020;**8**:1346-1361

[28] Daizhu Z, Haoquan G. A low-complexity steered minimum variance beamforming algorithm and its application on weak-target detection. In: IEEE 3rd International Conference on Information Communication and Signal Processing (ICICSP). Shanghai, China; 2020. pp. 194-197